The Church And The Black Man

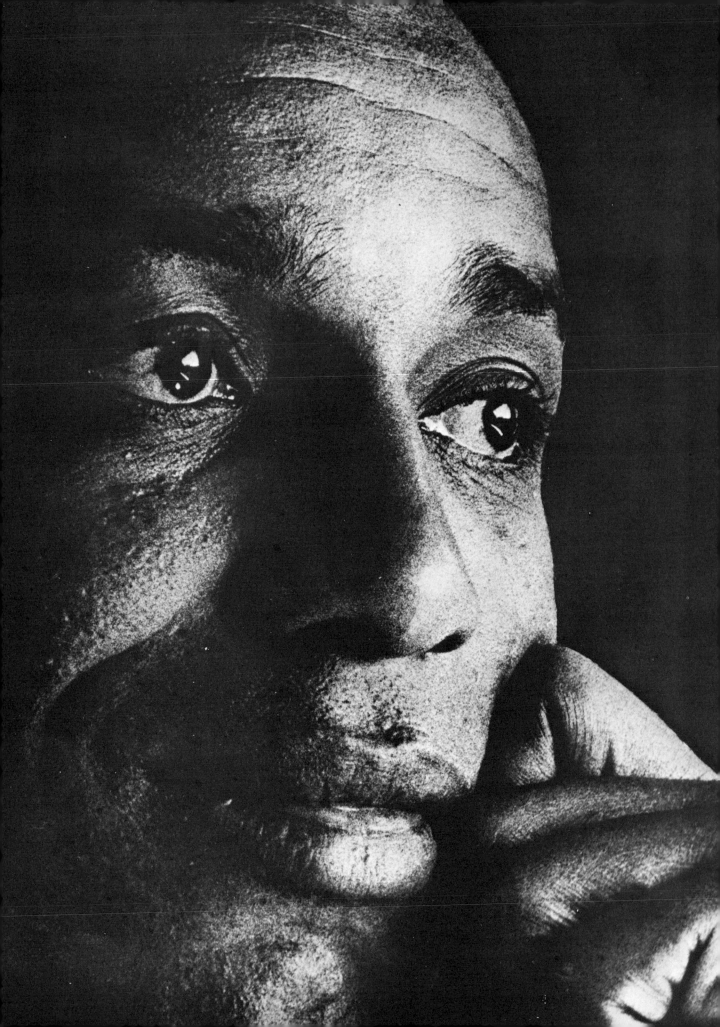

THE CHURCH AND THE BLACK MAN

as seen by
John Howard Griffin
author of
BLACK LIKE ME

Before we can have truth,
we must first eradicate
all traces of racism…

Pope John XXIII, Pacem in Terris

Pflaum Press · Dayton, Ohio 1969

Photo Credits

Cover, frontispiece, p. 21, p. 34, p. 38, p. 60, p. 79, p. 96 — JOHN HOWARD GRIFFIN

p. 10, pp. 14-15, pp. 66-67, p. 107, p. 109, pp. 114-115, p. 125 — WILLIAM F. PATTERSON

p. 73, p. 75, p. 81, p. 84, p. 87, p. 99 — UPI

p. 45, p. 101, p. 117, p. 121, p. 128 — JEFF LAWSON

p. 13, p. 29, p. 93, p. 97 — PAUL TUCKER

p. 46, pp. 56-57, p. 90 — WIDE WORLD

p. 26, p. 51, p. 133 — JAMES A. BAILEY

p. 41 — ALAN ODDIE

p. 4 — RELIGIOUS NEWS SERVICE

p. 2 — HATTIESBURG AMERICAN

Book design by WILLIAM F. PATTERSON, Dayton, Ohio

Photo selection by ALICE J. HUGH

Library of Congress Catalog Card Number: 68-55961

Pflaum Press
38 West Fifth Street
Dayton, Ohio 45402

To all of those, many of them my friends and colleagues, who have braved certain character assassination and probable physical assassination, in the cause of truth. Each in his own way knew and accepted in advance the terrible risks inherent in Christ's words from the Gospel of John:

All the demands that I make of you are this:
that you love one another.
If you find the world hates you —
and you will —
remember that it hated me
before it learned to hate you.

...more, the hour is now coming when those who kill you will claim to be serving God.

Trans. Gerald Vann
The Eagle's Word

CONTENTS

The Church and the Black Man   1

Some Painful Truths   16

The Good White   47

The Alternatives: What Next?   69

Epilogue 1: The Church and the Urban White   102

Epilogue 2: The Position of the Catholic Church
    in the Black Community   118

THE CHURC

ND THE BLACK MAN

The Church And The Black Man

On Passion Sunday, 1968, Dick Gregory and I walked with the campus minister toward the chapel of the University of the Pacific in Stockton, California. The minister briefed us on our schedule for the day. Dick Gregory would speak at the morning worship service in the campus chapel and I would speak that afternoon at Mass in a nearby all-white community.

Dick Gregory glanced up at the sunlit facade of the chapel.

"God, I hate to go in these pagan temples of hypocrisy," he said quietly.

Neither of us answered. There was nothing to answer. I remembered a scene in the kitchen of St. Carthage's rectory in Chicago where we talked through the night with a group of priests serving slum parishes. Dick Gregory told us how, as a youngster, he had sought refuge in Catholic churches. "I'd open the door and look in. If the church was empty, I'd go in and sit—just to get away from the noise and stink of the slum—just to be alone for awhile away from all that."

Now, the kind of edifices he had once considered places of sanctuary had become in his mind "pagan temples of hypocrisy."

We listened that Sunday to a liturgy that struck us as starkly personal.

"O God, sustain my cause, give me redress against a race that knows no piety, save me from a treacherous and cruel foe . . . ."

A voice sent the words out over wires and speakers in the church.

"Deliver me, Lord, from my enemies."

The glances we exchanged expressed clearly what we did not need to say; the "cruel and treacherous foe" for us was racism, quite particularly racism that hid behind the guise of religion. That cruel and treacherous foe had killed too many men and women whose lives had been connected with our lives.

". . . more, the hour is now coming when those who kill you will claim to be serving God."

Who would be racism's next victim?

Who would be the next to die physically from a bullet or a club? Or who would be the next to go through that kind of death that comes from calumny, character-assassination, blackmail?

I listened to the sounds of the service. I wondered if others heard the words of the litgury with the same personal recognition we did. Had any of them known the intimate grief of seeing friends and colleagues calumnied, shot or beaten by racists who called themselves Christians?

Dick Gregory, his bearded face skeletal from a long fast, looked at me and then leaned forward, his elbows on his knees, and stared at the floor between his feet. Was he remembering the victims? If so, which ones?

Father Morrisroe from Chicago who was

2

shot in the back in the same shooting that killed Episcopal seminarian Jonathan Daniels?—both men guilty of nothing more than acts of mercy, but dismissed as "nigger lovers" in Mississippi. Tom Coleman, their admitted killer described as a "good family man," was acquitted in a trial that blamed the victim, that sought to prove him a sinner and his executioner innocent.

. . . those who kill you will claim to be serving God.

Was it Vernon Dahmer, murdered when his home was fire-bombed in Hattiesburg, Mississippi, in a holocaust that injured also his wife and daughter. The victim was blamed. He was a black man guilty of seeking civil rights. Did the murderers claim to be serving God? Defense-fund benefit dinners were held for the accused killers and reported in the newspaper as "a tremendous success." According to the newspaper, tickets for the fund-raising dinners read: "Proceeds to defend our white Christian citizens being charged and persecuted under the so-called Civil Rights Act."[1]

. . . those who kill you will claim to be serving God.

Was it Chaney, Schwerner and Goodman, a black Catholic and two Jews, brutalized and executed near Philadelphia, Mississippi, after being entrapped in an act of mercy by a group of "white Christians," one of whom was a preacher who prayed before the three men were murdered?[2]

Page 4 Hattiesburg AMERICAN   Wednesday, February 28.

Dahmer case

Dinner March 9 to raise funds for 12 defendants

By RALPH HAYS

LAUREL — A benefit dinner to raise funds for the legal defense of 12 Jones County men indicted by a Forrest County grand jury in connection with the fire-bomb death of Vernon Dahmer will be held at 7:30 p. m. Friday, March 9, in Laurel's Pinehurst Hotel.

Mrs. Sybil Nix, chairman of the event and wife of a defendant, said the defense dinner is sponsored by the Jones County chapter of Americans for Preservation of the White Race. Mrs. Nix is chairman.

She said Clifford Wilson, the Laurel Jaycees' Distinguished Service Awards winner and one of the defendants in the case, is president of the chapter. He is charged with murder and arson.

Mrs. Nix said featured speaker will be Ace Carter of Jackson, manager of Jimmy Swan's gubernatorial campaign last summer.

Swan also is scheduled to speak, in addition to several others, said Mrs. Nix, who is wife of Deavours Nix, charged with arson in the Dahmer killing.

Cases of all the men are set for call next Monday, the opening day of the court term at Hattiesburg. Seven of the suspects are charged with murder and arson, the others with arson only.

Mrs. Nix said that the fund-raising dinner is not a Jones County affair but a statewide effort to raise funds.

A similar dinner was held cently in Jackson and Mrs. described it as "a tremend success."

She said that although Jones County organization only four weeks old, it alrea has 153 members. She said Campbell of Jackson is pr dent and will attend the La gathering.

Plans for the $10-a-plate ev will be discussed at 7:30 p. Friday at a special meeting Celeste's Diner in Laurel, M Nix said.

Tickets to the dinner read "Proceeds to defend white Christian citizens be charged and persecuted un the so-called Civil Rights Act

. . . those who kill you will claim to be serving God.

Was it Clyde Kennard, that brilliantly endowed black man who served in the armed forces of his country in Germany and Korea, fighting in defense of "American rights and liberties," and who then returned to his homeland, sought to claim just one of those rights—the right to complete his education—and was martyred by men who would call themselves good Christians. Dick Gregory had spent a great deal of money trying to save Clyde Kennard's life.

. . . those who kill you will claim to be serving God.

Was it Clark Cooper, Auburey Pollard and Fred Temple—beaten and murdered in the Algiers Motel in Detroit by men who, under the guise of love for law, order and virtue, reportedly said: "We're going to kill all you black-ass nigger pimps and throw you in the river," and who terrorized two women by stripping them, beating them and asking if they wanted to die first or to watch the men be killed and die afterward.[3]

. . . those who kill you will claim to be serving God.

Was Gregory remembering these, or the many others who have died in similar ways? Or perhaps, like me, he thought of those who have been martyred without being physically destroyed, including the priests, nuns, ministers and rabbis attacked for seeking to implement their churches' teachings on racism and justice.

I thought of the nuns who had gone to Selma, Sisters I had known in their convents before they went and after they returned from Selma. Catholic racists deliberately contrived "documented proof" in the form of spurious photographs purporting to show that the Sisters were not nuns at all but whores from New Jersey hired to masquerade as nuns. These photographs were distributed among Catholics by Catholics who had to know they were spreading a lie but who were willing to murder the reputation of Sisters.

. . . those who kill you will claim to be serving God.

I remembered sitting in a rectory one Sunday afternoon in an upper-class Oklahoma City parish with a young priest who had gone to Selma. His face blanked with disbelief as he told me of the animosity this had aroused in many of his parishioners.

"I never really believed men who seemed to be such fine citizens could be so enslaved by these prejudices," he said. "What's happening to them? I get hate stares now, right in church, from people who wouldn't think of missing Mass. This morning one of the ladies who had received communion from my hand met me at the doorway after Mass. She refused to shake my hand. She looked me straight in the face and asked, 'How's

The Black Christ by Devon Cunningham

4

your *woman,* Father?' It's been spread around that Selma was one big sex orgy. They're pretending we didn't go there out of conscience or for a principle, but because somebody promised us an experience with a black woman. What is all this? If these people were trash, you could understand it, but they're not, really. They have above-average educations. . . ."

Priests, ministers, rabbis, nuns, were deliberately calumnied by Christians who had to defend their racist aberrations with such *ad hominen* attacks.

. . . those who kill you will claim to be serving God.

Nearly all the churches have known these "old and ugly subtleties" as Adlai Stevenson called them, whereby men commit crimes of calumny and murder under the guise of religion and patriotism:

In Mississippi where 28 Methodist ministers appealed for racial justice and were attacked as nigger-lovers by their own congregations.

In Oklahoma where Catholic racists calumnied Bishop Reed with leaflets and a hate sheet.

In Milwaukee where Catholic racists calumnied Archbishop Cousins with newspaper ads and attempted to character-assassinate Father Groppi.

In Ferriday, Louisiana, where a group of Sisters came to work with black children, only to be called "whores" and threatened

with physical violence, guilty only of acts of mercy.

In Rochester, New York, and Chicago and St. Louis and Detroit and New Orleans where men have dared to exercise religious leadership rather than religious followship in dealing with racism.

The lists could go on and on.

Whose life would be taken next? Whose reputation murdered next?

Within a few days we knew. Martin Luther King was shot down on a motel balcony in Memphis.

It was not enough that his life was taken. Some men continued to murder his reputation after his death. Father Edward Grace, an American Augustinian priest, informed a service club in Galt, Ontario, Canada, that Dr. King, at the time of his death, was about to be apprehended by the F.B.I. for Communist activities. When consulted about this, the F.B.I. called it an "absolute falsehood."[4]

The words of a black priest, Father August Thompson, have guided me through the preparation of this book. "Yes, write it, John," he said when I called him for advice. "But for the love of God, please don't make this just another white man's book about black men. We've had about all of those we can stand."

Much of the following material, therefore, has been taken from taped interviews with *many* black men, and the book has been written in consultation with *many* black men.

I say *many* because I constantly encounter the suggestion from whites that black men think monolithically. White men often tell me what *one* black man or lady said to them, as though this represented the thoughts and feelings of all black men. I always advise them to ask the same question of twelve other black men, and suggest they will probably get eleven different answers. Black Americans no more think monolithically than do white Americans. The very suggestion that black people think monolithically is viewed by many black men as one of those revelations of unconscious racism that so falsify truth and handicap communication. It is an attitude that lumps human individuals together into a group and then attaches group characteristics: black men think this way; or, black men act that way; or, black people ought to think such and such a way.

Black men, experiencing it daily, understand it as a frustrating element of the duality of viewpoint that destroys all hope of communication. White men too often talk with a black man as though he were a combination Rap Brown, Uncle Tom, Black Panther, Baptist Preacher, Uncle Ben and Aunt Jemima rolled into one "culturally disadvantaged" package, which means white men are looking at him and speaking not to him as a human individual, but to a "group," not to attorney Wright, but to Negroness in general as conceived in stereotype.

This duality of viewpoint is a prime key to our difficulties. Lionel Trilling somewhere remarked that culture is a prison unless we know the key that unlocks the door. It is a first principle of anthropology that members of one cultural or ethnic group tend to regard those of another as merely underdeveloped versions of themselves. This is almost universal and it is fundamentally racist. Churchmen appear particularly prone to this error, which accounts for some of the ineffectiveness of missionary activity; or in cases where it is understood, accounts for some of the effectiveness of such activity. It helps explain why the recent Glock and Stark studies[5] revealed a higher percentage of racial prejudice among the churched than among the unchurched in the U.S., and how they could find that one-third of the clergy were racially prejudiced.

This problem of an imprisoning and blinding culture expresses itself in what Dr. Edward Hall calls "the silent language"[6]—a language by which men unknowingly express, through attitudes, springing from learned behavior patterns, truths that contradict their actual words, and of which they may be wholly unconscious. This silent language is an intrinsic element in the duality of viewpoint that

6 persists between black and white Americans. The duality is grounded in racial and racist mythology so deeply inculcated in learned behavior patterns that men tend to call it human nature, which it is not at all.

Black men meet this attitude constantly in encounters with even the best-intentioned white men who sincerely believe they are "all for the Negro," but who betray an illusion that blacks are underdeveloped versions of whites and must be helped to rise up to "our level." To black men, whose lives have forced them to become masterful interpreters of such nuances, this is so degrading it alienates immediately.

In a letter dated April 10, 1968, government investigator John Biddle wrote Archbishop, now Cardinal, Dearden, President of the National Conference of Catholic Bishops: "For over two years I have been travelling around the United States, attempting to determine if Negroes and other minorities are getting equal treatment in various governmentally funded employment and training programs. The chief lesson I have learned through many investigations, is the discrepancy between what is proclaimed as opposed to what is performed in behalf of Negroes. Most white Americans claim that they are in favor of justice and equality for Negroes, yet even while they are proclaiming this, they are depriving them of their God-given rights. The Catholic Church in the South is no exception in proclaiming integrated churches, yet at the same time neither welcoming Negroes to white churches nor preventing hostile laymen from keeping them away . . . .

"Thus the old system of dual churches — white and Negro — continues unabated in the South. In this age of reform and renewal in the Church in America, how can this blot on social justice be allowed to continue? Is this not an area of legitimate and immediate concern by the National Conference of Catholic Bishops? It is my sincere and strong hope that they will see the urgency of alleviating this scandalous situation in the immediate future."

On April 1, 1968, in a letter in response to Mr. Biddle's formal complaint about an incident in which a black Catholic was allegedly insulted for attending Mass in a white Catholic church in his archdiocese, Archbishop T. J. Toolen, Bishop of Mobile-Birmingham, wrote: ". . . there is no 'system of segregated churches' in this diocese, nor, to my knowledge elsewhere. Churches exist where by reason of past development membership is largely Negro. Members of such congregations are by no means restricted to such parishes by any official system or attitude. On the contrary, we have moved where possible to repudiate and correct any popular or unofficial practice that is an outgrowth of racism. I am not so sanguine as to believe that we have been totally successful in this, but change there has been and we will do whatever we can to continue in this direction."

Here we have the duality of viewpoint and the contradistinction between what is quite sincerely professed and what is practiced.

As white Catholics in the South, we were always taught exactly what Archbishop Toolen contends above: that black parishes existed for the convenience of black people, but that anyone was free to worship in any church. I believed that until I lived as a black Catholic and discovered another reality. Then I was simply told that I had to go to the nearest black church—and this could mean travelling for miles, even when a white church might be only a short distance away. I was repeatedly told: "Don't you dare set foot inside that white Catholic church." If there was simply no black church in the area, then we could attend services, seated in special places and acting with a special protocol. This is not a Southern phenomenon, it is racism in religion, and it is often practiced with at least the tacit consent of local church authorities.

In long experience, I have found only a handful of men who could break out of the prison (in this case) of an essentially white culture and who were capable of "thinking human" rather than "thinking white."

One of the reasons a black man might speak with contempt for "the white man's God" is because too often what he hears as the word of God from the white man's mouth comes into his ears as a distortion of the truths taught him by his own life. He hears the white man talk about a theological definition of man as a *res sacra*, a sacred reality, and this without regard to race, color or creed. But then, where this makes sense to him, he hears in addition and from the same lips, all the paternalistic equivocations that separate "our black brothers" from other men, stand them up as a group somehow intrinsically other, intrinsically different.

It is not a question of the black man's *judging*. It is a question of the black man's experiencing in his life the contradictories of discrimination in the very institutions that defined him as a sacred reality, and that moreover profess to abhor that very discrimination. He reads splendid statements signed by the church leaders; and he discovers too often that if priests seek to implement such statements, the same bishops who signed the statements suppress the priests.

These contradictories are overwhelmingly evident to black men, and they are deeply insulting because part of their implication is that the black man cannot see through them, or perhaps even does not perceive them. As a result we have a long history of alienation because of a compro-

8

mise that sought to avoid it. How many church leaders have warned against "pushing things too fast and in a manner that might alienate souls"? Black men used to hear that all the time; and black men wondered at the obtuseness of it—the Church's fear that by being what it professed to be, it would alienate souls. Whose souls? Apparently the souls of prejudiced whites. Black men saw through it. Black men saw that in going along with white prejudices, the Church apparently had little concern about the alienation of black men's souls. After all, there were the Negro and Indian missions; and weren't bishops always writing letters soliciting funds for missionary activities "among our beloved colored brothers." All of these implications told the "Sacred Reality," if he happened to be black, that he was somehow a different "Sacred Reality" from whites: they were churchmen while he still remained a missionary subject, not even counted in some of the church census-taking.

After a lifetime of such duality, and with the knowledge that it has gone on for generations, black men do not have very high hopes that white men will ever see clear in this. Because it is not new. White men appear to think it is new and contemporary, to judge from their appeals for patience on the part of the black man, and their judgment that "such things take time," and "you can't change men overnight." This is

again part of the duality. It is new to the white man, but it is old, old to the black man, who has heard these things all through his life, and back through generations. He knows that militancy is not new. Over a hundred years ago black men were saying it "like it is" and publicly and loudly:

"Your prayers and hymns, your sermons and thanksgivings, with all your religious parade and solemnity, are to him (the black man) mere bombast, fraud, deception, impiety and hyprocrisy—a thin veil to cover up crimes which would disgrace a nation of savages," Frederick Douglass said in a speech given in Rochester, New York, July 4, 1852.

I am not suggesting that churches ever really wanted it that way. Part of the tragedy we witness today lies in the fact that no one really wants what is happening, but the duality of viewpoint has become so extreme that we are virtually two groups of citizens in possession of two different sets of information, moving into deeper quagmires of incomprehension, with white perceptions about the problems of black men lagging far behind black perceptions. An indication of this is found in the nearly universal refusal of white men to contra-distinguish between militancy, black power and violence. White men use these terms almost interchangeably. Black men do not and never have intended for them to be used interchangeably. Most black men have been driven to a stance of militancy, some find solutions in black power concepts. Advocacy of violence or nonviolence is simply another thing, not relevant to the first two terms.

Again, none of this is new.

"Those who profess to favor freedom yet deprecate agitation, are men who want crops without plowing up the ground . . . . Power concedes nothing without demand . . . . Find out just what any people will quietly submit to and you have found out the exact measure of injustice and wrong which will be imposed upon them, and these will continue till they are resisted with either words or blows, or with both. The limits of tyrants are prescribed by the endurance of those whom they oppress." These words, which sound so contemporary and which express sentiments that so alarm men today, were spoken in 1857. They are from Frederick Douglass's West India Emancipation Speech.[7]

We miss the point completely if we go on thinking that these are new and recent developments. They are continuous and degenerating. Because man did not listen to Frederick Douglass and those like him a hundred years ago, we hear in today's streets, these statements:

"Some of our people still don't take that old blue-eyed, hooknosed picture of Christ off their wall—take it down and step on it. These people have been exploiting us for years."[8]

And: "When the time comes, it is going to be too late. Everything will explode because the people they live under tension now; they going to a point where they can't stand it no more."[9]

Or, as a young black man, with good cause, said to me last winter, in a rage meeting attended by his parents, fellow students and others from his community, "You go back, Mr. Griffin, and you tell your friend, Mr. Jesus Christ, and you tell your friend, Dr. Martin Luther King—shit." He had been grossly brutalized and subjected to injustice at the hands of local lawmakers, and no local white religiously-identifiable person or group had uttered a word of protest.

Anyone working to bridge the gap of incomprehension brought about by this duality of viewpoint faces an almost hopeless task. White men will think he is exaggerating, black men will think he is understating the truth. White church leaders will reprimand him for not "stressing the good things the church has done." Here the implications are dizzying. They can range anywhere from the belief that "we took them out of the jungles, civilized them, gave them a religion and helped them to progress," through the belief still taught in some schools "that everything good that has happened to the black man has been thanks to the white man's generosity," and on to

the authentically good things that in fact the churchmen have done. The illusion that "we know better" is so profoundly engrained in us that even when black priests point out the contradictories which so afflict black men and of which they have such profound knowledge, they appear not to be taken seriously, and I have seen letters in which some are reprimanded for "insolence" and for "daring to question" their bishops on these matters, and are told that the Church is not answerable to them.

As Father August Thompson, a black priest, remarked recently when he was chided by white religious colleagues for "stepping out of line" by telling it too bluntly and by black men for telling it too mildly, "Blessed are the peacemakers, for they will catch it from all sides."

Part of the current disillusion has come from white leadership's inability to disabuse itself of this "we know best" syndrome. Many of us have gone on and on talking with religious and civic leaders over the years, analyzing the difficulties that could lead to fratricide, and being dismissed as "unduly pessimistic"—sometimes only a few weeks before the community exploded. And after the community exploded, the "we-know-best" syndrome remained intact because community leaders simply refused to see the true causes and began to look for the Communists and "traveling black agitators who came in and stirred up our good black people." Sadly enough, such men really believe that the explosions had to come from outside causes. A first principle of racism holds that you always blame the victim. Black people, knowing intimately the situation that causes such explosions, are plunged into profound disgust at the suggestion that some outside Communist or black agitator had to come in and tell them that they were in an unhappy situation. They cannot believe that white leaders really believe this and feel that it just another case of the white man's finding a scapegoat for his own community's deficiencies.

The Church long ago talked about the problem as one of "white racism." The Kerner Commission spoke of "white racism." Both were ignored, and massively. Devout Christians who were prejudiced felt that the bishops had suddenly stopped leading and started meddling; just as later they were to complain that the Kerner Commission report "blamed everyone but the rioters," which is rather like suggesting that we should blame the powder keg for exploding when the match was tossed.

All of this has led to a kind of *a priori* distrust fatal to any real dialogue. This distrust has bewildered white men who have dedicated themselves to justice. Ironically, but understandably, such *a priori* distrust is strongest toward such men, because too often they are the ones involved in en-

12 counters with black men in which these unconscious attitudes spill out in ways that they never recognize but that are always recognized by black men. Too often they assume the lead, they speak before listening, and then when they are ready to listen the black man has said: "What's the use?"

Hopefully the alarm and the discontent felt by both blacks and whites over this duality of viewpoint can lead to its solutions.

But the hour is late and all the concern in the world is not going to help so long as the same fundamental errors afflict us, so long as churches go on trying to convert black men not to Christianity (many are already Christians) but rather to a Christian kind of whiteness—obviously a self-defeating hypothesis. Still today, even at high levels of religious and educational leadership, too many continue to talk about "bringing them up to our level." I do not mean to imply that this is done with malicious intent or that it is in any way insincere. No, it is simply that these concepts are so deeply inculcated that even when men deny them intellectually—as many now do—their language and their attitudes go on expressing them in a way that degrades black men.

Until a fundamental reorientation occurs, white men, again with the best intentions, will offer—no, insist upon—solutions that are irrelevant to the black man's lived experience and his own perception of his needs. Seemingly good acts will merely alienate black men further.

This fundamental reorientation will begin to occur when white men come to the profound realization that black men simply do not want to become imitation white men or imitation white Christians. Black men can only judge by the evidence presented. The view that black men have of white men is quite different from the view that white men have of themselves. Conversely the view that white men have of black men is quite different from the view that black men have of themselves. With this duality of viewpoint, unbridged because of difficulties of communication, black men have found little about white men that they want to emulate or that they want their children to emulate. The first evidence of this reorientation will become apparent when white leaders, dealing with problems of concern to black men, or to both black and white men, seek consultation with black men— when black men are included in the highest levels of decision-making processes, and consulted deeply and authentically. Only then can we hope to avoid subjecting black men to those same old solutions based on the white man's white interpretation of problems that afflict black men. More importantly, only then can black men function as truly self-determining citizens and churchmen in helping find solutions that have true relevance and actually make sense to black people.

To accomplish this requires a profound understanding of the imprisoning aspects of culture, a willingness not only to be open to other concepts and values but to respect them. Sarah Patton Boyle, after long and deep struggles, could finally write that she had at last escaped "the prison of my whiteness," in her biography, THE DESEGREGATED HEART.

These deeper perceptions, which have taken so long in coming and are not here yet, nevertheless are more and more evident.

What many thought was a simple problem has now been seen in some of its complexity and explosiveness. Changes at this profound level are evident and growing. Because they are not so well understood, they are often opposed by men still too deeply calcified in the "we-know-best" syndrome, who dismiss what they do not understand as merely idealistic or impractical and who apparently ignore the massive evidence that their concept of "the practical" and "the prudent" has not prevented us from making a shambles of justice and approaching the brink of fratricide.

Some Painful Truths

We have lived under two damaging delusions in this land. First, the delusion of southern white men that we knew everything about what we patronizingly called "our Negroes," and that no outsider could possibly understand.

Second, the delusion in nonsouthern areas that "it's not like that here."

We still hear widespread expressions of both delusions. These expressions come from perfectly sincere white men. No black man believes either of them, of course. The experience of blackness gives the lie to both delusions.

The patterns of such delusions are clearer in the South and they shed light on the more complex ones of nonsouthern areas.

Great numbers of southern white men had a similar formation, often within the heart of the churches.

Many of us, as small children in the South, had contact with black people. Some of us were allowed to play with black children. Great numbers of us had the experience of being reared with the help of a black lady. We felt certainly that we loved her better than almost anyone we knew.

But when we reached a certain age—usually six or seven—society rather than our parents necessarily, told us that the time had come when we must alter these relationships. We must stop playing with black children. We must enter into more reserved relationships with the black lady who had helped care for us. We were made to understand that this was the good, the kind, the proper thing to do. Society maintained that black people preferred it that way and that we would embarrass them if we acted otherwise.

In essence, as small children, we had the experience of intimate and loving contact with black people and later of being separated from them. The memory of our early affection remained intact even while we were being taught to view black people as "different." This is why so many southern whites can talk about "how much we love our Negroes," even while deeply implicated in permissive suppression of black people.

These patterns, so obscure to most whites, have been clear to black people. The black lady who cared for the white child, who diapered him and bathed him and surrounded him with love was aware that he would grow into that structure that so impeded her own children's ability to function freely as men. This has been one of the secrets shared by black people. When I was black, it hurt us to see white children clutching at the skirts or hands of parents who loved them and who, without ever knowing it, would cooperate with a system that filled them with racial prejudice.

These learned behavior patterns combined to form in southern white children a concept of fellow human beings as "intrinsically other." We came to look on pigmented human beings as totally and mysteriously different from us, having different needs, different aspirations, different responses to stimuli, different moral values.

We were told that only "white trash" would be unkind to black people. As "good whites" we had to understand that "our Negroes" were just racially and ethnically different from us, childlike and "inferior," through no fault of their own, and we had to understand and love them as they were, all in taking certain precautions to keep them in their place.

As white children we were dimly aware that the trash did frightful things to black men and women. We heard rumors about the sexual mutilation of black men at lynchings. We heard about the large crowds that sometimes attended public lynchings, about mothers who held their children above the crowd for a good view. The delusion that we were not prejudiced was strengthened in us because most of us were not at such lynchings; we were in our homes, hearing our parents and grandparents lament such monstrousness.

We failed to perceive the obvious: that racism had dehumanized the racist even more than it had dehumanized his victims, that the racist himself was clearly racism's most tragic victim.

The rest of us, the "good whites" were not, we told ourselves, prejudiced. It wasn't a question of prejudice. It was simply that black people were intrinsically other. Other groups were intrinsically other, also. Look at the Jews: it was better never to trust them. Look at the Catholics: a foreign-based church with God-knows-what kind of designs on this fair land. Look at the French, a civilization mostly Catholic and utterly without morals. They were all intrinsically other, but they were white and not intent on raping our good white women the way black men were. So, as long as black men stayed in their place and did not rape white women, their morals in their own community were not our concern. And we knew that a major part of their "intrinsic otherness" lay in this absence of sexual morality, and that this was an ethnic characteristic. They were just "naturally less moral" than we whites.

This is one of the keys. We have not begun yet to face this painful truth: the atmosphere of our youth was permeated with sexual myths about black people. Even if our parents tried to protect us from such myths, or sought to make us question them, society hammered them into our ears.

These myths told us that "you were not really a man until you had a black woman," that if you wanted to change your luck, you got a black woman. It was massively conceded that sexual contact with a black woman was far less sinful (if at all) than with a white woman. It was widely believed

18 that the most pernicious danger of the white youth's contact with the black woman lay in the probability that he might never find a white woman sexually satisfying in his later life. It was the doctor's or the churchman's duty to warn white adolescent males of the danger of this addiction to black flesh: the implication being that the black woman, without moral refinement, greatly enjoyed animalistic sex and that a man need not have with them the reticences he must have with decent (even sacred) white womanhood, and that therefore no white woman could ever really compare to a black woman as a sexual partner. On the other hand, the same men warned us of the sexual brutality of the black man, his dream of possessing the white woman's flesh, the constant risk of rape for white women unless a firm hand was kept on the black man.

Such myths are not regional, as non-southerners would like to believe. They exist all over this land. When I lived as a black man, white men frequently asked me if I would not like to possess white women. And today white men ask confidentially if I heard much talk among black men about their desires for white women. Students everywhere, obviously having heard this and not really wishing to believe it, ask me if it is true that black people want "integration" just so they can have white women. Recently when I was discussing com-

munications problems with a group of Catholic Sisters who ran a school in Chicago, one of the Sisters asked how they should handle the problems of black children's sexual manifestations in the school.

"The same way you would handle white children's," I said.

"Well, that's what I would have thought," the Sister said, "but one of the priests said we should just overlook it because 'they' were just naturally that way."

"Whereas 'we' are not?" I said.

"Well, that was the implication," Sister said with a painful laugh.

God and sacredness have always been the terms evoked—and made the equivalent of whiteness. Thus racism was perfectly structured from the white man's viewpoint. Black women were essentially helpers, caring for the white children, cooking, washing; and at least potentially sexual objects. If, on the one hand, a black man touched a white woman, it was considered catastrophic. The very heavens cried out for vengeance and demanded his death in reparation for the taint that would forever mark the white woman. On the other hand, if a white man touched a black woman, it was merely a sign of human weakness. Certainly it was not an act that merited punishment.

In all of this, the underlying justification rested firmly on the illusion that fellow human beings were "intrinsically other." Once that was established, all the other illusions followed, including the one that said "they like it that way."

The final result was a whole and complex structure of racist mythology, an imprisoning culture of white racism from which few could escape. We were given a distorted view of man the moment we came to see him as intrinsically other.

This view manages to emerge from most cultures: first the concept that members of another culture are intrinsically other; followed by the concept that the "other" is an underdeveloped version of ourselves.

We have not yet seen this as the crime it is—the crime of inculcating early in children a false and distorted view of man; planting it so early and so deeply that even if in later years the child should correct these errors at the intellectual level, he can remain emotionally entrapped by them. Black men are constantly affronted by men who are intellectually liberated from prejudices but who remain emotionally entrapped by them, whose words are sincerely antiracist but whose attitudes remain racist. As a result, the whole of society is damaged, not just the obvious victim group. The society that consents to these errors rarely perceives the damage done to its own prejudiced children.

To suggest that churchmen are immune to these errors is to misunderstand how early and how pervasively they are formed

in us by society. Most theologies agree to a basic definition of man as a *res sacra,* a sacred reality. This has nothing to do with race, color or creed, but with man. The moment that some men, for whatever reasons, consent to regard other men as less than sacred realities, they have said yes to a racism, no matter how seemingly benign, that can lead to almost limitless evil. Training in philosophy and theology should help men to recognize and understand such errors—especially since most of the argumentation by which men justify racism and deny their prejudices constitutes a catalogue of traditional fallacies of logic. But prejudice exists at such irrational levels that men who can handle reason splendidly in other aspects of their existence, often respond emotionally, viscerally, irrationally, and indeed seem impervious to scientific data, in the one area of a deeply held prejudice.

In any event, the distortions were seldom corrected by our church leaders who suffered the same handicaps, the same delusions of deep affection for black people, the same benevolent "understanding" that *they* were different and could not be judged by white men's standards. Sometimes white men were given straight talk about their abuses of black women, but this stressed the damage done to the sinner, not the damage done to the sinned-against black lady. Rarely did the minister penetrate through the curtain of prejudice, because all the evidence, all the facts and the justifications and rationalizations were too perfectly structured to permit this, even if he could have glimpsed the other side of that curtain and seen what the truth was for the black man.

The extraordinary minister who did try to clarify conscience in these matters was usually battered with reprisals, called Communist and mongrelizer and nigger-lover, thrown out and replaced by a "real Christian with the right kind of religion." If the minister were a priest, he might be accused of the same things, with the addition that he was "imprudent," and he might be silenced or suppressed.

Black men are deeply percipient of the contradictories between what the churches profess in their condemnation of racism and what is actually practiced in the way of harrassing and suppressing priests and ministers who attempt to implement the churches' teachings in these matters.

Critically involved is the question of customs and traditions that have been hallowed by time. This exists everywhere. It is neither southern nor contemporary. We remember the lines from Voltaire's *Zadig* in which Zadig protested the ancient custom of having wives hurl themselves on their husband's funeral pyres, particularly in cases where the wives showed no enthusiasm for this joint immolation.

" 'But,' Setoc said, 'women have had the privilege of burning themselves for more than a thousand years: who amongst us would dare alter a law thus hallowed by time? Is there anything more worthy of respect than an abuse dating from ancient times?'

" 'Well,' Zadig answered, 'reason is more ancient still.' "

Certainly, priests and ministers of any religious denomination who have attempted to correct racist attitudes and practices have been subjected to society's (and frequently their own denomination's) demands that they respect abuses "dating from ancient times," hallowed under the term "our customs and traditions." Both Fathers Ouellette and Joyce, during their Alabama sojourns, were reviled by coreligionists, for disturbing "our customs and traditions" when these two priests sought to implement their church's teachings on racial justice. A generation earlier, Fathers John LaFarge, S.J., John Markoe, S.J. and William Markoe, S.J. were harrassed and insulted for the same reasons and in the same terms. Father John Markoe was referred to as "Nigger Markoe" by a fellow priest who later became a bishop. Similarly, Rabbi Charles Mantinband was too outspoken for Hattiesburg, Mississippi, and was replaced by a man "more interested in purely scholarly matters and not so concerned about social issues." The list of

Fathers William and John Markoe, Jesuit pioneers for racial justice.

such men is long. It includes men all over this land. Local bigots protested them. The silence of men who should have supported them, including their own hierarchies, was interpreted as a condoning silence—a silence condoning their persecution.

The same kind of condoning silence has surrounded racist groups that cover themselves in the paraphernalia of religion and patriotism.

Sam Bowers formed his White Knights of the Ku Klux Klan in 1964 to "discourage" civil rights advocates. This most violent of the Klan groups has been implicated in ten murders and countless acts of brutal intimidation, which they call "Christian Violence." Bowers justified this violence in a widely quoted "theological" explanation written in 1964.

"As Christians we are disposed to kindness, generosity, affection and humility in our dealing with others. As militants we are disposed to the use of physical force against our enemies.

"How can we reconcile these two apparently contradictory philosophies, and at the same time make sure that we do not violate the Divine Law by our actions which may be held against us when we face that Last Count on the Day of Judgment?

"The answer, of course, is to purge malice, bitterness and vengeance from our hearts.

"To pray each day for Divine Guidance that our feet shall remain on the correct path, and that all our acts be God's Will working through our humble selves here on this earth.

". . . Our Father's Law tells us not to mix the seed of His Chosen White Race of Israel with the seed of the beast.

"This is the Law, but the Baal-worshippers of Satan's Synagogue insist that it must be all right to mix the races because a money profit can be made doing it. Since their money is god, and they do worship their God religiously, they simply cannot see anything wrong with mongrelization, and therefore regard Christian White Supremacists as fools, fanatics and law-breakers."

I am not, of course, suggesting that many men agree with this mentality, or that this is typical. No, on the contrary, many men, including Bowers' own father, repudiate this stance. Even so, what many repudiate is the extremism involved in such a stance. They will not say the big yes to this kind of extremism, but they will go on saying the smaller yeses to less extreme expressions of the same racism, all in persuading themselves that, by comparison, they are not bigots. It is the smaller yeses and the condoning silences that allow society to maintain a permissive repression of fellow citizens who happen to be "other," whether black, brown, red or whatever.

Though we shrug off with contempt the

extremist expression of racism, it can have its effects unless it is squarely repudiated. It is dangerous to dismiss the hate-mongers as ineffectual trash. Racism, unrepudiated, that begins against any given group, quickly spreads to encompass other groups. The Klans were not only anti-Negro (no matter how they denied being anti-Negro or cited cases where they took food-baskets to "good Negroes") but anti-Catholic and anti-Jewish as well. After the killings of Schwerner and Goodman, Sam Bowers is reported to have expressed his satisfaction because this was the first time that the execution of Jews had been successfully planned and carried out in this country.

One of Sam Bowers' recent followers was Mrs. Kathy Ainsworth, a 26-year-old college graduate and schoolteacher in Jackson, Mississippi. She appears to have been an outstanding teacher, a person of stability and dedication until she gradually became poisoned by hate materials. These came to her not only from the White Knights but also from an anti-Semitic organization known as The Church of Jesus Christ, Christian, which operates out of a post box in Lancaster, California. This organization was founded by a disciple of Gerald L. K. Smith, a man named Wesley Smith who once worked with Father Coughlin. Mrs. Ainsworth, under the influence of such racist propagandists, finally came to national prominence when she was slain by the police while attempting to dynamite the home of a Jewish businessman in Meridian, Mississippi.

Freakish, yes. An isolated incident, yes. Perhaps not, however, when her death was so mourned and others promised that "this dedicated Christian will not have died in vain."[10]

These incidents and attitudes are widely known in the black community—such things have made up the history of the black man in America. They are nothing new. What is new and desolating is that white society now talks about racism and denounces it; churches and educational institutions issue splendid statements, but society still maintains an almost permissive indifference to crimes of white racists.

On the other hand, white society is fervent in its demands that black men be brought to justice. Recently, in Maryland, I was questioned about the possible effects on the black community of bringing H. Rap Brown to trial. Would this crystalize black sentiment in favor of Mr. Brown? I pointed out that so long as society was not equally fervent in demanding that men like Sam Bowers be brought to justice, then the trial of Mr. Brown, who so far has done nothing but talk, would certainly crystalize black sentiments, not necessarily in favor of Mr. Brown, but against white men and their concepts of justice. This kind of duality, which is so widespread, has long since

24 brought black men to despair of a cure for white racism.

This is part of what black men call "the System." The system, in this sense, might be defined as that whole complex of customs and traditions that have been passed down in their abusive as well as their good aspects, and that have all the strength of law, plus local discriminatory ordinances.

The system has always told black men about themselves. For example, the system has told black men that they are citizens and as such they should pay their taxes and defend their country from its enemies. That part of it is splendid. No one could ask for anything better. However, suppressed minorities have learned to wait, when society says a good thing about them, because that good statement is too often followed by a qualifying term like the word "but" after which society says what it really thinks.

So, what the system really says to black men is that they are citizens and as such should pay taxes and defend this country against its enemies;

but black men should not vote (in some areas);

but black men should not have equality of educational or employment opportunities;

but black men should not have equality of protection under the law;

but black men should not be fully self-determining;

but black men should not have equal access to those culturally enriching elements that allow the human personality to expand and become fully functioning—concerts, theaters, schools, libraries, churches.

This list of *buts* could go on an on. It differs in its details in different localities. In some areas of the South, black people still find reprisals if they attempt to register or vote. In other areas where no one would think of denying black men *this right,* there is still the denial of the right to own property, to make housing loans or business loans. The very courts of justice which should be free of this duality still discriminate in a harsh and paternalistic manner. Too often they appear to regard the black man, no matter what his age, the way some parents regard their adolescent children who must be taught a lesson. Bail bonds for black arrestees tend to be higher than those for whites on the same kind of charge. Detroit attorneys Cornelis Pitts and Dean Robb recently referred to "the shame of a two-faced legal system—one for the whites and one for the blacks." Negro litigants in civil cases often receive substantially lesser verdicts while in criminal cases they receive harsher sentences. One of the symptoms of white racism as read by black men lies in this: whites who today might very well protest discrimination in eating places, seldom appear to see such discrepancies in justice even when they are made public.

In any event, the system, no matter what its local characteristics, refers to this whole set of contradictories faced by black men in a society where norms are established by middle-class whites. American white society would find it intolerable to be ruled by an ethnic group other than itself. American black society finds it equally intolerable.

The system not only does not make sense to black men, it is deeply persecuting and frustrating precisely because white America imposes the set of contradictories without perceiving what it is doing, without *experiencing* what its effects can be.

The white church, without desiring it or intending it, is part of the white society that imposes the system—or at least that has not understood how to clarify and rebut it effectively. The black man can judge only by the evidence presented to him. Some of the evidence has been excellent. The attitudes and activities of Fathers Lafarge, Markoe, Shocklee, Mottet, John Smith, Coffield, Merton, Groppi, Dunne, Twomey, Morrisroe, Seminarian Jonathan Daniels, Rabbi Mantinband, Rabbi Heschel, Rabbi Levi Olan, Duncan Grey, Sarah Patton Boyle, Matt Ahmann, Emil Seliga, Rev. Reebe, Will Campbell—to mention only a handful of religiously identifiable whites from among hundreds who deserve mention, have been curative and

encouraging to black men precisely because each sought not merely to help the black, but to help all of society in the area of human justice, and because each of them saw the tragedy of the white racist, as well as his victims, and saw also that the Church too often went along with him (out of fear of alienating him) but did not cure him.

"The racist is the greatest challenge the church faces today in both the North and the South," observed Will Campbell. "One might say that he is the true adolescent of adult Christianity; the most unlovely and the most in need of love. Certainly the church must not tolerate what he stands for, but it must not abandon him in its attempt to force him to maturity. . . .

"I have seen and known the resentment of the racist, his hostility, his frustration, his need for someone upon whom to lay blame and to punish. I know he is mistaken, misguided, and willfully disobedient, but somehow I am not able to distinguish between him and myself. My sins may not be his, but they are no less real and no less heinous. Perhaps I have been too close to this man. Perhaps if I had not heard his anguished cry when the rains didn't come in time to save his cotton, if I had not felt the severity of his economic deprivation, if I had not looked upon his agony on Christmas Eve while I, his six-year-old child, feigning sleep, waited for a Santa who would never come; if I had not been one of

him through these gales of tragedy, I would be able to condemn him without hesitation. If I had not shared his plight, if I had not lived with him in an atmosphere of suspicion, distrust, ignorance, misinformation, and nefarious political leadership, surely my heart would break less when I see him fomenting mob violence in front of *his* schoolhouse and *his* church house. Perhaps I would not pity him as much if I were not from his loins. But pity him I do.

"But the church must not pity the racist. It must love and redeem him. It must somehow set him free. . . ."[11]

In the early sixties, when the above was written, many black men would have agreed with Will Campbell, because black men have had these insights for a long time.

Today, because white racism has spawned black racism, a black man could write the same lines in explaining his concern for the black racist. Alas, most white people would not agree with him the way black people would have agreed with Will Campbell.

All of those religiously identifiable white men listed above, and indeed many others, understood these truths profoundly. That is what distinguished them from the mere do-gooders who, with the best intentions, burdened and offended so many black men precisely because they tried to "raise" the black man up to their level.

28 Churches give the impression that they are "white" rather than human-divine because too often, all in condemning racism and injustice verbally, they do not make clear the distinction between loving the racist and refusing to tolerate what he stands for. Churches, in fact, frequently give black men the impression that they tolerate very well what the racist stands for.

This is why black priests, who love the Church, could be driven at last to refer to it as a "white racist institution" after black men in the streets had been calling churches that for a long time—and with overwhelming evidence that is simply not apparent to white men. The fact that such evidence is not apparent to white men does not in any way nullify the fact that it is painfully apparent to black men.

The recent funeral of Leander Perez, with full Church honors, in a chapel on the campus of Loyola University in New Orleans, shocked some black men into saying it was the last straw. It scandalized white men, too, since a number of white priests objected.

Perez, an outspoken racist, longtime political power in Plaquemines Parish, had been excommunicated by the late Archbishop Joseph Rummel for his opposition to Catholic school integration. According to Archbishop Philip Hannan, Leander Perez was reconciled with the Church more than a year prior to his death and the reconciliation "followed the procedure established by canon law."

"The censure was imposed because of opposition to the authority of the Church," Archbishop Hannan said. "The absolution from the censure involved a public statement accepting and supporting the authority of the church. This statement was made publicly over a year ago on March 8 at a ceremony at Fort Jackson before a numerous group. The fact that it was not reported by the press does not affect the case and is a matter of the freedom of judgment of the press."

In a letter dated March 21, 1969, six priests wrote the Archbishop:

"Respectfully, but firmly, we wish to register a strong protest concerning the burial of Judge Leander Perez from a Catholic church. In all candor, we consider the event a disgrace to all right-thinking persons, Catholic and non-Catholic alike. The leading racist of the South was buried with full and solemn honors in a Christian church, on the premises of an important Catholic educational institution, with the leading figures of the racist world assembled there under one roof during the Mass, sacrament of unity and brotherhood.

"To those who say that Christ was more forgiving, we say that Christ forgave those who were repentant, who repaired the damage they did to the persons of God or man. To those who say that Judge Perez was in

30 fact reconciled to the church some 18 months ago, at which time the excommunication was lifted, we say that this is a mere legalism. If a man continually affronts a large number of our citizens in front of the television cameras, then he ought to make restitution in front of those very same television cameras; he cannot make up for a public insult by some private prayers or token penance. In the eyes of our society, Leander Perez represents, even at this very moment, a racial position absolutely irreconcilable with the Christian religion.

"To those who say that no one of us is without fault or sin, we say that tolerance of the weak is a virtue. But here we have not merely a man influenced by the inescapable traditions of his upbringing, but a man who has carefully built his career on principles, on a way of life, clearly opposed to fundamental teachings of the Gospel.

"To those who say we cannot pass judgment on any man, we say that we are not passing judgment. Leander Perez could be a saint in the eyes of God, according to his own conscience. Nevertheless, what he says and what he publicly stands for is in no way in accord with the beliefs of the Christian religion. Since this is true, let us say so and act accordingly.

"To those who say we must have regard for his family, we say that we can pray with them, have Mass among them for Leander Perez, but in private, in their home, not as a public ritual of acceptance. To those who say that, after all, Christian burial is only a symbol, we say that it is a symbol that speaks all too clearly a message we are not sure should be communicated—to the Negro, to those whites who have given two or five or 20 years to the work of equality, justice, respect— a message which says, 'It doesn't really make any difference what you believe or what your goals are.'

"Archbishop, does the Catholic Church in the South stand for racial respect and justice, as we have been telling people? If Leander Perez had been a Mason, he could not officially have been given Christian burial. We ask, is Masonry more opposed to the essence of Christianity than racism, the preaching that one group of human beings is intrinsically and necessarily inferior to other human beings?

"If Leander Perez, as a Catholic, had been living in a bad marriage, according to Catholic law, he could not officially have been given Christian burial. We ask, is living in a bad marriage more serious than giving one's life to the public promotion of distrust, suspicion, hostility, and the constant teaching that one race is somehow less worthy of respect than another?

"When men without any religious faith at all are preaching decency and concern for brotherhood, where does that leave us in the Catholic Church, who are caught in the act of publicly honoring as one of our members a man who is a racist?

"What does the black community think of us at this moment, as organized religion appears to betray them once again. How do our white citizens who are sympathetic to racial justice now feel, those who may have at some time jeopardized career or social standing for principle, confident that the Church stood beside them? How do our Catholic schoolteachers feel when their instruction, so often negated by parents or pastors, is now so definitely neutralized? Will they not say, Archbishop, as we feel compelled to say, that the institutional Church has done it again: sought peace at the price of principle, acted with supreme caution at offense to no one, looked like its stands for nothing?

"Expressing ourselves to you with fraternal regard and respect, anxious to criticize with affection and charity the Church we want to have force and meaning in the modern world, we ask that as aftermath to this serious and dangerous mistake you announce in the clearest possible terms the commitment of the Catholic Church without reservation to the cause of justice, respect and love among all men, all races, all nationalities, and religions."

The letter was signed by six Dominican Fathers: Gilbert Roxburgh, theology department, Loyola University; Richard Trutter, associate pastor, St. Anthony of Padua Parish; J. A. Nadeau, theology department, St. Mary's Dominican College; Kilian Downey, Michael Duffy and Mel Buechele, all of the Xavier University theology department. According to Father Roxburgh, their letter was by no means the only one expressing dismay.

It is clear that, in the Perez incident, the Church loved the man, as is right, but it failed to repudiate his racism and thus gave the appearance of tolerating it, even of honoring this symbol of racism. This not only disturbed black men and white men devoted to the cause of justice, but it must have reassured and comforted many racists by giving an impression of tacit consent to Perez's notorious racism. Those who protested did not object to Perez's return to the Church, certainly not to the Church's willingness to love the man "influenced by the inescapable traditions of his upbringing"—they objected to the Church's seeming failure to find his racism intolerable.

Unfortunately, this is only one example from a long history of such examples. If it were new or unique or merely regional it would not be worthy of mention. Why do the organized churches appear deaf and insensitive to the needs and appeals of black men? Black men have spoken and spoken from deep knowledge. Should not the organized churches begin to realize that black Christians, especially priests, are not being merely perverse and insolent in these outcries? Black priests especially realize how tragic and deep now is the black man's distrust: their cry is that we not go on in this terrible waste, that we understand the contradictories of the "system," that we correct at profound levels the whole concept of the "intrinsic other."

"The hard core of social hostility which has so often erupted into overt acts of discrimination and violence is fortunately found only among a minority of Catholics, albeit an all too vocal minority," wrote Father Jerome LeDoux, S.V.D. "These are the Catholics who cannot find it in their heart to eat beside a Negro; no, not even to worship their common Maker beside one. They are those ushers who shepherd dark people to the last seats or right out of the church, usually with the connivance and sometimes with the blessing of the pastor. Those are the Catholics who rise up from the communion rail and refuse to communicate because of the advent of a Negro communicant. Yes, they are also the priests who turn their back on such a communicant without giving Holy Communion; who pretend they are not at home when a dark visitor rings the doorbell; who fawn upon their own color but greet the others with a tangible coldness. . . .

"You may be tempted to brush the whole messy question aside by blaming 'the people.' . . . What attitude could 'the people' be expected to take if so many priests and,

in some cases, even bishops treated Negroes as if they were lepers?

". . . I think it is now more than obvious that we have squandered the prime conditions for true mass conversion of the Negro. He was thrown only crumbs at the time when he hungered most for the true word of God. In many cases now, before being offered that word, the knowledgeable or prosperous Negro will first have to be jarred out of his distrust and new feeling of self-determination. This does not mean that we should give up the chase, but rather that we should redouble our efforts."

Father LeDoux goes on to make a point that preoccupies many black men.

"The saga of the Negro and Catholicism has often been underscored by a reversed leadership. Too often it was a lay magazine or a lay speaker who cried out for moral wholeness, for charity, for justice. Too often, it was even the secular press dragging a silent clergy in its train. Most dismaying of all, the Church has been a tail-light in the very issues in which leadership should justify her very existence. The civil courts have demolished many barriers which the church by divine obligation should have disposed of long years ago. Too often certain leaders crept behind civil ordinances and crowed, 'Me too'! Can you imagine anything more incongruous than being allowed to eat where you want before being allowed to worship where you want?"[12]

In line with this, last Thanksgiving, 1968, the local white Catholic church in a small Louisiana community, Ferriday, held an "ecumenical" service. All the community's white Protestants were invited, a white Methodist minister was the main speaker; but no black Catholics, not even the local priest, were invited. The black priest, Father Thompson writing in protest to the white priest, stated: "To show you just how brutal the facts could look when pushed to their actual underlined reality, I would like to offer some prayers that could be offered in thanksgiving on such an occasion.

" 'O God, we thank you that those infernal long arms of the Federal Government that have made us accept anyone of your children into OUR schools and OUR places of accomodation, regulated OUR voting laws, told us how we may not sell OUR houses, etc., cannot force us to take a Christian stand in Your House.' "

Harsh words from the pens of black men, yes. What whites do not appear to realize is that the experience of blackness is everywhere crammed with this kind of incident and has been so for a long, long time. What the white Christian does not often perceive is the terrible feeling of attrition that these attitudes drag on and afflict black people—not so much in their immediate effects, but in the cumulative message that black Christians are still regarded as *"different"* or *"intrinsically other."* This is the maddening part. Whites sometimes state that black men want "special treatment." Father August Thompson answered that black men have had special treatment all along in the churches and want simply to have normal treatment as men, as children of God.

Father LeDoux also makes the crucial point that much of the heroism of the advocates of justice simply should not have been necessary in the first place.

"Happily, the past was not all shadow and bungle. There were the Cardinal Ritters here and there. There were the giants like Father LaFarge, who labored untiringly with pen and the spoken word to arouse the slumbering conscience of a nation. There was also the occasional pastor who went completely out of his way to guarantee a measure of charity and justice to the minorities. Self-sacrificing Josephites, Blessed Sacrament Sisters, Holy Ghost Fathers and others set the pace which our Savior Himself would have set had He been here. The pity is that these relatively few individuals did work created not so much by a lack of laborers as by a positive neglect on the part of the laborers. In other words, for all the generosity and devotion of those religious, their work should have never been necessary. Canon law tells each pastor that he has a grave obligation to

care for *all* the souls within his parish boundaries."

Again, Father LeDoux gives the solemn warning that cannot be repeated too often apparently—the warning that these are not regional matters and that "they do happen here." The system destroys men, destroys a sense of dignity and manhood. Whites, with no comprehension of the reality of the system and its destructiveness tend to look on damaged black men, say they got that way by racial or ethnic characteristics and use this to justify the perpetuation of the very system that created the damage.

"Even highly intelligent people can be guilty of ridiculous inferences in this regard. Witness the white minister's statement in the *Saturday Evening Post* (April 10, 1965), to the effect that desegregation would ruin the social structure of rural Mississippi. Really, is the social structure of rural Mississippi something worth keeping? Lest northerners read such things and thereby feel they are not so bad after all, let them remember that this identical argument, however implicit, is the one which fired riots in respectable places like Cicero, Illinois; which gives wings to the feet of whites when a single Negro family plans to move in; which prompts the withdrawal of 'exemplary' Catholic school children faced with the prospect of colored schoolmates; which inspires the common workingman to wax eloquent on sundry injustices until a man of color tries to enter his union."[13]

A sense of urgency permeates the statements of black men today, including those of black priests and nuns. They have seen the tragic waste and have seen that attitudes, though changing, do not change in pace with the black man's reality. "The Negro's patience has not just worn thin in these matters," Father LeDoux observes, "the skin is all gone."

It is this time-lapse between white society's perceptions and the black man's reality that has become so crucial. Black parents, realizing the damage done to their children, particularly their male children, because men simply do not seem able to give up or heal their racism, say "How can they go on asking us to watch our children being ruined just so they can go on indulging their prejudices awhile longer?" Black parents see this as massive fraud committed against them by white societal attitudes. They see it simply as one group of citizens, handicapped by racism, cheating against another group of citizens—nothing less.

Somehow, white society, hopefully helped by religious leaders, must break through and begin to see these matters as black men see them—for the salvation of the total society and quite particularly for the salvation of white America. This

36

is not meant threateningly. Black men have long said and deeply believed that it would be up to the black man to save this country from its racism. Black men have about given up on that, finding that racism deeper, more pervasive than even black men had believed. Black men are "giving up" on the white man, the white man's Christianity and his white-dominated institutions. This may mean the salvation of black manhood, but it also may mean that white society will carry that much longer the burdens of its injustice, its impercipience, the terrible wastefulness of this country's murdered dream.

While we are concerned with "telling only the good things," black men have been telling the things that make us unbeautiful in the hope that these will be corrected and we can talk about the "good things" without feeling so callously selective.

In 1964, black priests expressed themselves in an article compiled by Father Rollins Lambert of Chicago, published in the November issue of *Sign* Magazine, "Negro Priests Speak Their Minds."

Nineteen percent of the black priests interviewed said that their superiors had interfered with their speaking or writing on racial questions.

Many expressed embarrassment in the matter of explaining church practices to potential converts. Many black people,

especially those interested in the church, are aware of the wide discrepancies between what the churches profess and what they tolerate in practice.

"We need more Negro priests and religious. The Church's mission to the American Negro—if we are really serious about it—needs them. Our 'changing' city parishes need them. But Negro youngsters (particularly girls) are still encountering color bars at the gates of their religious vocations.

"One superior told a girl I know that the community to which she applied, already praying desperately for new vocations, would pray to the Holy Spirit to guide her *somewhere else.*

"And there's a parish school in Chicago where the Sisters dare not talk about religious vocations for girls lest a colored girl should perhaps be attracted to their own order.

"I think it is fair to say that the local— not official — failures of parishes and institutions to be open to everyone are the main obstacles to the conversion of the educated, professional class of Negroes. They know about these stupidities. They will not accept attempts to explain them away. If I've heard it once, I've heard it a thousand times: 'The Church's stand on divorce and birth control are well known; in these matters the Church permits no equivocation. Why isn't the Church's teaching on charity equally well known to Catholics? Why is it not enforced?'

"Heartening to many Negroes was Archbishop Rummel's excommunication of two white Catholics for resisting desegregation. But other Negroes still ask: 'Only two?'

"There is now every indication that the Negro is going to attain his objectives—equal employment, housing, education, dignity within the next decade or two. He will reach them with or without the Catholic Church. If he reaches them without the Church—after all the struggle and humiliations, the police dogs, the cattle prods, the beatings in the streets—what can we expect his attitude toward the Church will be?

"We Negro priests can sense when you are patronizing us. We can detect your secret bias, secret even to yourselves. We are weary of all your cliches. A well-intentioned white man once loaned me a book of poetry to be quoted in sermons because, he said, Negroes have a natural sense of poetry and rhythm. I should have said I also flip over watermelon.

"What do Negro priests want? They want to build a million bridges between man and God, between white and Negro, between Catholic and Protestant. It's a task only for a man who is not afraid to be alone."

Some random statements from black priests in different parts of the country:

"A Negro priest feels he could do more for the solution of race problems, but the diocesan authorities do not seem aware of what problems there are, or what to do about them."—Northeast.

"I am proud to show that the priesthood is not above my people, but I also feel my position has relegated me to the sidelines in the great moment of my people's history. I strongly suspect that superiors have not yet recognized any particular obligation to develop the Negro priests' potential for maximum impact upon society."—Midwest.

"There is absolutely nothing for a Negro priest to do in this town as far as recreation is concerned. The white priests are okay, but I have been here several months and have not yet been invited out even one time by them."—South.

"Once I was rejected by a white priest. He would not accept my services to fill in for an absent priest. And this was in Indiana, not the South!"—Midwest.

"Never too comfortable. People want and expect you to be mild. The priest must also hear the inner sense of inferiority of other Negroes. There sure is plenty of hate around. And why don't Catholics confess all those sins of racial hatred?"—Northeast.

"Those two words—'Negro' and 'priest' —when combined, spell personal tension to me. He meets staring and unbelieving

eyes, once in a while from a face with hate or a smirk. I see Catholics lined up to receive Communion from my hands, and yet they get up and pout when a Negro layman kneels down beside them."—Northeast.

"It can become a very lonely life. The greatest frustration comes from bishops and priests who seem to run from the chance of being seen in public with a Negro priest. You are always hoping some priest will say, 'The hell with it all; let's be priests for a change, regardless of your being a Negro.' "—South.

"If the Church in the South could be really 'Catholic' we could really change in ten years. It is a hell of a job when you can't get fellow priests and bishops to understand."—South.

Now, six years later, many changes have come. From the point of view of white Christians, these changes appear edifying, from the point of view of black men, the changes have not actually produced change, not fundamental change. Almost every one of the above statements would remain the same or become harsher if spoken by the same men today. Black priests have virtually been ignored in their desires to "build a million bridges between man and God, between white and Negro, between Catholic and Protestant." The sense of aloneness has not changed except that now black priests have mitigated it

somewhat by closer association and communication wth one another. Black priests who find it necessary to be more and more plain-spoken are still too often admonished by white colleagues who have not yet seen the point, not to push so hard, to "tone it down," to be patient; never understanding that "the Negro's patience has not just worn thin in these matters; the skin is all gone."

Until white men, particularly white churchmen, can gain some perspective into the profound and crucial validity of the black man's viewpoint, the situation will continue to degenerate. The black man is pinned down by the "system" in ways almost impossible for the white man to perceive. White men hear black men, for example, cry out about loss of manhood, loss of dignity, the need to be self-determining. They hear this from black men who appear to be virile and masculine and they never understand what black men actually mean. Black men on the other hand cannot believe that white men do not understand and their anger increases.

To oversimplify this one point, which is typical of many such points, the system with all its contradictories, simply prevents black men from functioning fully as men in ways that are absolutely necessary for a man to function if he is to have any self-respect. This occurs in four main areas:

A man must have the dignity of being

40

a stable breadwinner and a breadwinner with dignity. The system has arranged it so that the black lady has traditionally been the more stable income-earner: she has always been employable. The man, if he had a job, could not hold it with any dignity. When I was black, we would start out to work in the mornings saying: "We've got to go out and climb our mountains of yeses, and grin, grin, grin," or "we've got to put on that white man's mask." No matter what injustices a black man suffered on the job, the moment he ceased to "grin and say yes" he was considered a "bad Negro" and risked losing his employment (or worse) immediately. So, if a man wanted to hold his job, he had to do it too often at the expense of basic human dignity. The system has denied black men the pride of being the real breadwinners and the pride of being breadwinners with dignity.

A man must have the dignity of being the protector of his women. The system has simply prevented the black man from this right until recently. White men abusing black girls and women have traditionally gone free, or have been able so to threaten their victims with reprisals that black people were powerless to seek justice. Black parents have always been concerned with protecting their girl-children from white men. Black men know that their mothers, their wives, their sisters, their daughters get the insults from whites,

and too often black men have to swallow this knowledge and writhe in agony—an agony of self-contempt. The system has traditionally not made it possible for black men to be the protectors of their women, something every man has to be in order to have any respect for himself as a man.

A man must have the dignity of feeling that he can offer his children something better. Black parents know the way they have come and under the burden of the system too often feel a terrible despair that their children must come the same way and that they cannot find the way to protect their children from the degenerative pressures of surrounding racism. Black parents know that the damage starts early, the moment the child perceives that he is being viewed not as himself, a human individual, but as the "intrinsic other." They know that the child is in for a lifetime of standing in front of doors that have to be open to all men, but that may very well be closed to him, not because of himself but because others regard him as the intrinsic other—doors to places of learning, to places of healing, to places of worship. The parent knows that the male child will early in his life lose the image of the black male as fully man, fully capable of achieving dignity and self-determination. He knows that in school the child will conclude that all the heroes in history have been white. He knows that all of this will

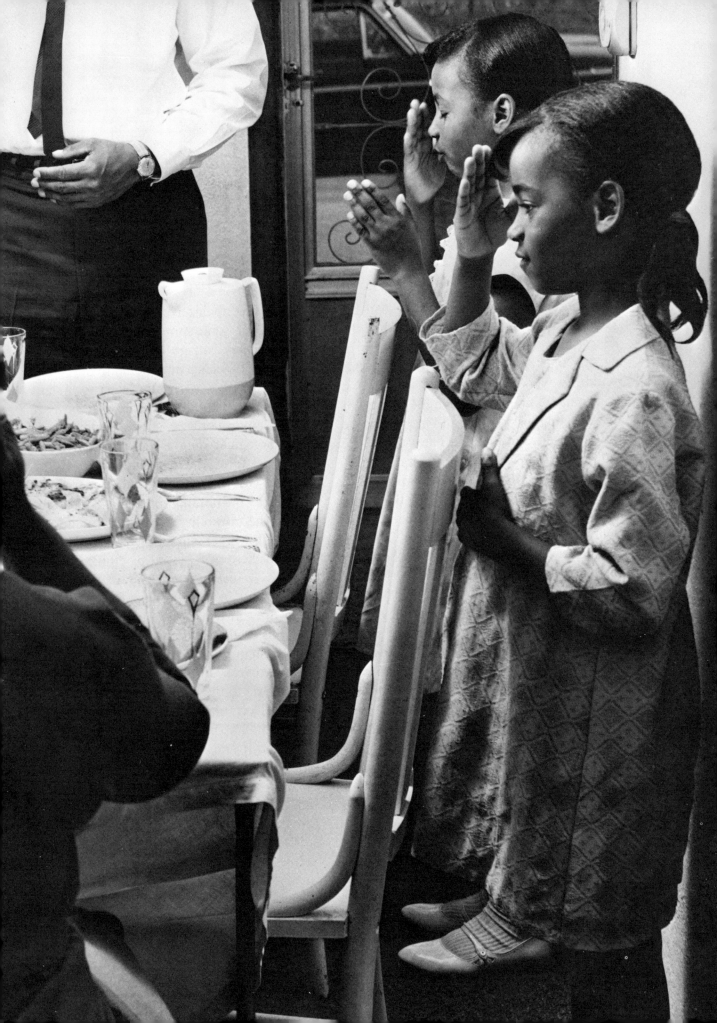

42 dim the child's vision of what he can become as a black male. So as a father the black man is deprived of the dignity of feeling that he can make it better for his children.

Finally, a man must have the dignity of determining his own life and his future: he must be self-determining. The system, the power structures of white-dominated institutions, in fact, constantly determine and delimit him in this matter. It is the white who decides whether he, the black man, will attend the local ecumenical Thanksgiving service. It is the white, not the black man himself, who determines whether the black man can attend a retreat in a "white" retreat house. "A Negro priest can attend the Forty Hours devotion in a white parish where the presence of a Negro layman would provoke cries of outrage from priests and people," wrote one of the priests in the *Sign* article. Similarly in all other activities, whether right or wrong, whites determine almost everything for black men, to the great distress of many black men.

So, in these four areas basic to man's ability to function as a man—as breadwinner with dignity, as protector of women, as provider of a future for children, as self-determining individual, the "system" has prevented black men from functioning as men. After a lifetime of this, and seeing that a lot of superficial changes have not altered the basic damage, some men simply

cannot face themselves any longer. Seeing no way out, some simply fail to come home because they can no longer bear the self-reproach of being in a home and yet not being the man of the house. The system has castrated the black man exactly as it would any other man subjected to it.

Sociological data is drawn from these patterns. Whites, even scholars, study the data or view the evidence and, understanding little or nothing of the causes, talk about the instability of family life and the frequency of common-law marriages (as though these were racial or ethnic characteristics), feel strengthened in their prejudices and in their conviction that black men are "instrinsically other." They then use this as the excuse for perpetuating the very system that has created the damage.

This cycle, so obscure to most whites, is intrinsic to the lived experience of blackness. Even black men who have been spared its harsher realties know it and understand it and are burned with rage as it continues.

This is one of the reasons black men resent not only the overt redneck bigot but are learning to resent even more deeply what in the old days were called "good whites." The good whites, on whom so many black people counted, have not understood in sufficient numbers the core problems of "the intrinsic other" and "the system" and have therefore failed to repudiate them and their deadly effects on black men. The "good institutions"—the schools and churches and hospitals and courts—have not, after all this time, seen deeply enough to come forth with the profound dynamism needed to bring fundamental change:—to cure racism and remove its taint from our highest institutions; to secure justice without any racist modifications; and most basic of all, to repudiate distorted views of what constitutes man in his essence, thereby lifting from black people, the psychologically murderous burden of the "intrinsic other" concept that exists massively as the foundation-stone for the whole structure of racism.

We are not yet near such fundamental change. Worse, despite the chaos that causes us such anguish, we appear not yet convinced of the desperate need for such change—for the salvation of all of humanity.

We still hear daily, often from important churchmen, the suggestion that if all rights were immediately restored, chaos might result. What do they think we have now?

We still encounter overwhelming evidence, in the media and in our churches, halls of state and courts, of that prime racist principle: "blame the victim."

We still find white citizens affronted because, having restored to black citizens a portion of those rights which this country guarantees equally to all citizens, black men have not fallen on their knees in gratitude; but, on the contrary, express growing bitterness that we continue, through complicity, silence and fear, to withhold any of them at all.

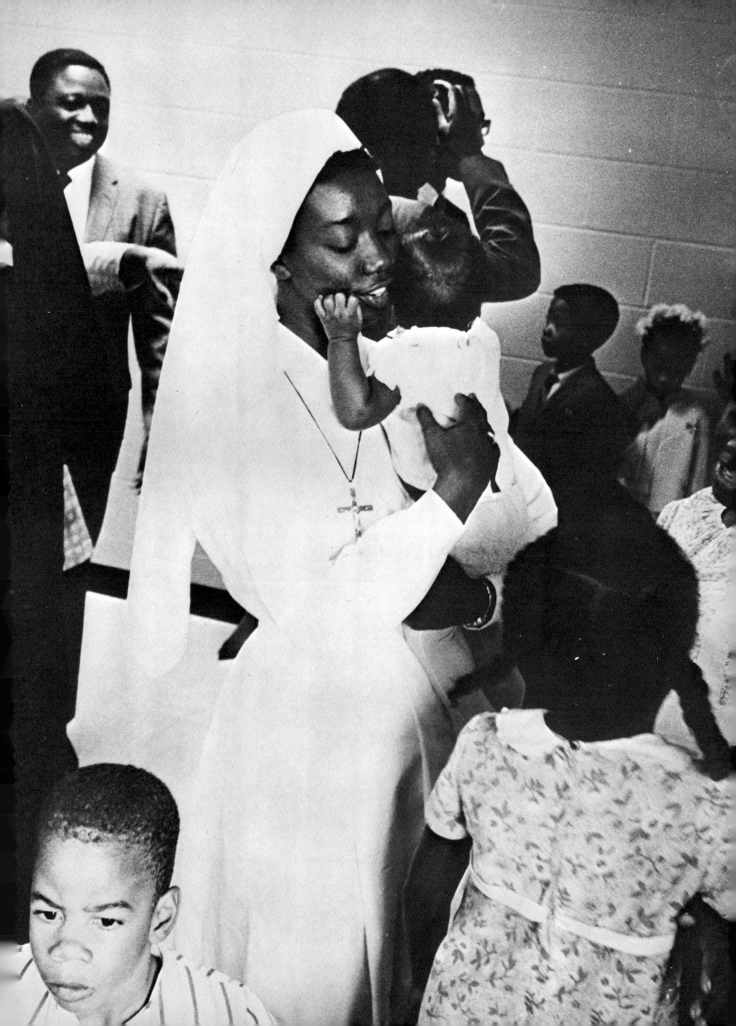

The Good White

Ten years ago a great reservoir of *a priori* forgiveness existed in the black world. Black men still spoke of "the good white" with affection, hope and gratitude.

The "good white" was that man or woman in the community who gave some evidence of concern for truth and justice and who appeared to understand that things were not right. The good white— the minister, teacher, doctor, lawyer, newsman or housewife—somehow got the message back to black men: although they could not do much at the moment because of reprisals from their own white community, when the time came, they would be the ones to stand up for truth and justice. Good whites, usually religiously identifiable men and women, were a safety valve of hope. They were silent, but they were known by black men in each community.

In the black world we talked about such persons, identified them. "They can't do much now, but when the time comes. . . ."

Even before the time came, a handful spoke out and took the consequences. Lillian Smith, the great Clarence Jordan, newsman P. D. East and others. They stood as heroic symbols of "the good white." Archbishop Rummel and later Archbishop Hallinan spoke and acted at a time when it took great courage, and they did it without equivocation. They reinforced the black man's belief in "the good white."

Then the "time" came: Little Rock, Clinton, Mansfield and other cities where racism flamed openly.

With rare exceptions, the "good whites" on whom black people counted, remained silent and invisible. It looked to black people as though racists were having a field day, unchallenged and unrepudiated. The term "good white" was heard less frequently. Black men began to believe that the good white was like all the others. He talked well in private but he did not stand up for what he professed to believe. Black men were bitterly disappointed that at least the institutions remained silent and invisible. The churches generally found it "imprudent" to speak out in time of crisis. The black man saw clearly what whites did not see: that in a racist society, nonracist whites were as unfree as black men. A Mrs. Peabody could come into the South as a symbol of this country's dreams and promises and end up in the jail. Lillian Smith had long ago warned us that we were "Killers of the Dream." Society and its institutions proclaimed the Dream of justice and equality but considered any individual who sought to implement the Dream a trouble-maker and probably a subversive. In the name of the Dream, we jailed the Dream.

Sarah Patton Boyle wrote from a Florida jail, "John, the time may be here when we have to produce white martyrs to prove

48 to black Americans that there is such a thing as a sincere white man."

Where, at least, were the churches, the identifiable men of God? A Duncan Grey stood up at Oxford. Twenty-eight southern Methodist ministers stood up in Mississippi—and were repudiated. Fathers John and William Markoe and Father La-Farge and others cried out. But they were too few and too often such men were suppressed by their own church leaders—or at least attempts were made to silence them. In general, religiously identifiable men were silent and invisible. It would have been helpful if they had done nothing but stand visibly and weep at the sight of racists beating up black women and children.

But their voices, addressed to black men, were heard by black men. They preached "patience" to the black man, and they went on preaching patience long years after Martin Luther King had told the people of Montgomery:

"For many years we have shown amazing patience. . . . But we come here tonight to be saved from the patience that makes us patient with anything less than freedom and justice."

Because churches at the national and world level issued statements condemning racism and injustice, black men had hope in the ability of religion to understand and bring cures to white racists. The great hope of black men in those days lay in the conversion of the white racist. The white racist justified his racism under the guises of patriotism and religion. It was hoped that the religion he claimed as the erroneous justification for his racism would correct his errors and cure him.

In practice, however, despite national and world policies, at local levels all over this land black men were faced with what could only be interpreted as equivocation in the churches. The very religions that denounced racism and all of its ramifications, still at local levels, gave black men almost constant evidence that the intrinsic other concept prevailed. The tragedy of this lay in the fact that most such churches had no intention of doing this and were unaware of the symptoms that black men interpreted: simply a *difference*, indicated frequently by oversights: the black child not solicited as an altar boy the way the white child might be; sermon references about black people that were not checked for accuracy with black people and therefore appeared to miss the point to the listening black men; support of the *idea* of fair housing without its implementation within the parish or diocese; the call on people to do out of "goodness" what should have been insisted upon out of justice; constant references to "the race problem" rather than the problems of racism; erroneous implications that the problems of racism were problems of black men rather than problems of the whole society; references to "your problems" (as black men) rather than references to "our problems" simply as men, because black men have always understood that the problem of racism concerns the total community, that it poisons the white child as much as it does the black child.

These and hundreds of other such nuances indicated to black men that the churches, all in espousing a theology that repudiated the "intrinsic other" concept, in fact continued to address black men as though they were "intrinsically other," allowing stereotype images to spill out in language and attitudes. Black men interpret these things. It is not a question of developing skills in semantics. Black men know that such linguistic and attitudinal errors would simply not be there, would not exist, if the distortions in men's view of what man is were corrected at their source.

It is in the foundering of men's highest hopes that the deepest alienation occurs. Quite unaware of what they were really saying, most churches adjured black people to patience and expressed the fear that by implementing their own teachings too rapidly, they would risk "alienating souls." Black men would have understood their refusal to abandon white racists. They should not, of course. But black men did

not see much concern over the alienation of their souls because, in the black man's experience and view, the churches, while loving the afflicted white racist gave the unfortunate appearance of at least condoning his racism.

Black men were sometimes driven away or frozen out of "white men's churches," or heard of others who were. Black men became wary of using the term, "good whites," and to speak with contempt—the contempt that covers profound disillusion —about "the white man's God." It was not from faithlessness or shallow faith, but from deeply wounded faith, that black men began to hurl challenges to white Christians to put up or shut up.

Since most white churchmen had neither undergone nor even perceived the damage experienced by black men within their churches, they tended to view the black man's reactions as perverse, or at best "unchristian."

However, many white churchman did see the contradictories. How often in the most racist areas have I heard anguished white churchmen ask "When is the church going to *act*? When is the church going to stand up and be counted?" Such men founded church-affiliated organizations for the purpose of standing beside black men.

Too often such organizations had self-defeating weaknesses.

In some cases, the whites, no matter how

50 concerned and well-intentioned, could not rid themselves of concepts of the stereotype and of "the intrinsic other." It was the old problem of sincerely seeking solutions to a disease while being tainted unknowingly with that disease. The smaller organism carried the virus of the larger organism, not wanting it, fighting against it, but possessing it. I have been asked by such well-intentioned people who were having their first black couple for dinner what kind of food they should serve black people and how it should be prepared. I informed them that black people were not only capable of eating "white food," they might very well be affronted if, out of a false sense of propriety, the white couple should serve fried chicken and watermelon. I also gently warned them to be wary of the other elements of the stereotype that can so offend black people—the idea that all blacks are educationally and intellectually disadvantaged, the idea that all blacks have a "god-given" sense of rhythm, are marvelous dancers, have superb natural voices, love only spirituals and jazz. This is an extreme, though true, case. To black people it will not seem as extreme as it will to whites, because black people encounter it in various guises in white people who belong to these organizations.

In some cases, the organizations were self-defeating because involved whites did not see the problem of racism as afflicting white as well as black society. Black people see racism as "the white man's problem" and as damaging to the total society. Black men are simply overwhelmed by the number of whites who want to do something "to help the poor black," with the implication that this is a "Negro problem" and that it involves somehow bringing the black people up to our level. This kind of myopia is diminishing, but it is still massive.

In some cases the organizations were self-defeating because it is the nature of organizations to feed on results, tangible and demonstrable results. When such tangible results failed to materialize quickly enough, discouragement set in. Some drifted into a state of attrition or became simply groups held together by personal friendships between blacks and whites, producing intangible results of great value.

Finally, such organizations were self-defeating in the sense that their nature prevented the black man from functioning as a self-determining factor. Religiously affiliated organizations usually had to clear their activities not so much with black men as with white hierarchies. No matter how wise, how committed, how benevolent such hierachies might be, or how encouraging and supportive, this meant that white men, somewhere along the line, still made the decisions and these decisions most often did not depend upon

deep consultation with black men but were based on a broader spectrum of church policy and politics and upon expediency considerations. This is not necessarily a criticism. It is a fact and no matter how justifiable or sensible, because of it black men were not truly self-determining in the decision-making processes of these organizations.

Disillusioned black men began to look elsewhere toward religions that would not affront men in their dignity as men. Religious organizations like the Black Muslims began to grow rapidly in membership. Younger black students in colleges and high schools would ask, "Isn't it true that perhaps Christ is for the white man and we blacks must look toward Mohammed, the prophet of Islam?" Our explanation that the damage came not from Christian ideals but from the mutilation of Christian ideals by men who professed Christianity, had little effect. The burns were too deep. Black men did not see that we would come to the light in the near future.

Much of our actions and attitudes as Christians simply indicated that our parochialism as "white Christians" was entrenched to a hopeless degree.

At a time when "white Christianity" was in low repute among black people, I was frequently asked to speak before mixed audiences, whites, blacks, Protestants, Catholics, Jews, Muslims. Often I would be introduced by a white Christian leader from the local community who spoke like the president of some religious chamber of commerce about how Christianity was our only hope and how only Christians could bring us out of this mess—a fairly tactless claim when the Jewish people present and the Black Muslims were doing at least as much, if not more, in bringing solutions to the deeper problems. Invocations were usually offered by Christians. In one city the invocation was to be offered by a Catholic bishop and the concluding prayer by a Jewish rabbi. Before going on stage, the bishop, an irrepressibly jovial man, told us "nigger jokes," which he thought were marvelously funny. I thanked God no black man was backstage to hear them, and I dreaded what he might bring out in his invocation. He gave a splendid invocation. I was interested afterward in the rabbi's remark that this was "the first such function I ever attended where an invocation was offered that did not affront my religion."

In those days of the late fifties and early sixties a spontaneous contradistinction was made between the "white man's Christianity" and the "black man's Christianity." This contradistinction implied among many blacks and many whites was that the white man's Christianity was not deep enough, strong enough to make him "be" what he professed; whereas the black man's Christianity, exemplified by men like Benjamin Mays and Martin Luther King was deep enough and strong enough to produce heroic action and the redemptive effects of unearned suffering.

In those years, black Christians demonstrated to the world a determination to save this country through love. Nonviolent resistance—not passive resistance—was the keyword; nonviolent resistance that might "bring about a transformation and change of heart,"[14] said Martin Luther King.

Black Christians by the millions responded to a call for what amounted to heroic charity. Nonviolent resistance challenged black men to love their oppressors until those oppressors were cured of the terrible sickness of racism, healed and liberated from the need to oppress others. At the same time it called for implacable resistance to discriminatory injustices. It loved the racist while refusing to cooperate with his racism.

If a black man drifted toward hate, he was warned: "Don't let them make you hate because then they will have dragged you down to where they think you are. If they can make us hate, they have won." Black men believed prophetically that only the racist would benefit if hatred were hurled against hatred.

One of the ironies of history will be seen in the fact that nonviolent resistance, based on the principle of passing through the Beatitudes in order to arrive at beatitude, anchored in the redemptive power of unearned suffering—was suspected of being "subversive" and called "communistic" by white Christian racists who were unable to distinguish between a Communist principle and a profoundly and essentially Christian principle.

Black Americans placed hope in an authentic Christian solution. They believed, they marched, they prayed, they sacrificed, they sang, they took the beatings and the spittings and the cattle prods and went on praying for their abusers—those white citizens who called themselves Christians and patriots. We cannot doubt that such men sincerely believed themselves Christians. They could only view as "dangerous" and "subversive" this deeper manifestation of Christianity by which black men sought to convert them.

Any man, white or black, Protestant, Catholic, Jew or whatever, who opposed their racism could be certain of character-assassination, attempts to impugn his sexual morality, economic reprisals, rumor campaigns that he was a "Communist" or "Communist dupe" or "pinko-intellectual." Question-begging epithets—the repeated use of certain terms long enough and loudly enough in the certainty they would finally make an impression on the unreflecting mind—were standard tactics: call

54 a man commie, say he advocates "mongrel-ization" and "race-mingling," repeat end-lessly that intellectuals are either "pseudo" or "pinko" and it produces its effects. This tactic of labeling a man Communist be-cause he was simply a nonracist became so rampant it led Lillian Smith to remark that it was high time we stopped giving the Communists credit for every decent, brave, courteous and courageous act committed by man in regard to racial justice.

Christian racists ravaged the Bible, and still do, in attempts to find supportive statements.

Most Christian racists, unable openly to defend racism, sought, and still do, reputable-sounding reasons for maintain-ing racist suppression: usually spurious economic or marital reasons. "Would you want your daughter to marry one?" This led P. D. East to remark that an estimated seventy-five percent of black people in Mis-sissippi had white antecedents somewhere along the line, but there had never been an "interracial" marriage in the state, probably to the grief of most of the children born of such unions. Black men said they were not eager to have their daughters marry white men either, but no black man had suggested that any white man be denied his rights as a citizen out of fear the white man might want to marry his daughter.

The duality of viewpoint was painful in the naivete of these attempts to find repu-table reasons for the perpetuation of dis-reputable racism. At a higher level, the concept of "rights and responsibilities" be-came fashionable. Even theologians would argue from the premise that "rights and responsibilities go hand in hand: until Negroes learn to live up to their responsibil-ities as citizens, they cannot be expected to have their rights." Everywhere business-men, teachers, preachers, community lead-ers adopted this principle to justify with-holding rights until it was pointed out that no one suggested that any white man be denied his rights until he lived up to his responsibilities of citizenship, and that in fact it was largely the white man's refusal to live up to such responsibilities that was causing all the difficulty: that these "rights" were guaranteed and protected for even the most degraded white man whereas they were still denied black Ph.D.s.

In a nation that vaunted itself as being founded on the principles of Christianity, white men and black men learned that it was patriotic to be "sensibly Christian" but somehow subversive to be "absolutely Christian." This is so deeply engrained that at the time of the publication of the Kerner Commission Report great numbers of white men, including government leaders, appeared disappointed in the Commission's failure to find any evidence of "conspir-acy" or subversion, and quickly lost inter-est in the report's recommendations.

In these years, some men were bewildered by the split between the "liberals" and the "conservatives" in this matter of racism. One concerned conservative wrote me in distress. "I am not a liberal but I promise you I have as deep a concern about racism and its injustices as any liberal. The way people are talking, the way writers are writing, you would think you had to be a liberal to have concern for justice."

Of course he was correct. The criteria of justice are objective, not subjective, and therefore should have nothing to do with a person's liberal or conservative leanings. Justice demands rendering to man his due. To render him more than his due is not justice but liberality. To render him less than his due, no matter what are our subjective reasons, is simply injustice. Since the objective criteria of justice are not met when modifications are introduced, how can men speak of "moderate justice"? I suggested to this correspondent that conservative and liberal alike should be thundering for justice and thundering against anything less than justice, because anything less is simply injustice. Injustice always involves injury of some sort. Commutative justice demands that what has been taken unjustly be restored: so justice in relation to victims of racism involves not only rendering to man what is his due as man, but also restoring (or making every attempt to) what has been taken from him

—his manhood, his self-determination, his educational and economic opportunities— all those rights that inhere in being man and without which man cannot function as man.

Black men often read white men's "theologizing" about racism, whether liberal or conservative, with justifiably jaundiced eyes.

Often men, liberal and conservative and "moderate," who know how to reason, have a good method, are competent theologians in the traditional sense, utter perfectly-reasoned idiocies when they address themselves to the problems of racism. The liberal may offer solutions and judgments that have no relevancy to the black man's lived experience. The conservative and moderate may decry racism in general but denounce specific means of overcoming the very racism they decry. We remember Father L. J. Twomey's remark about the magnificent courage shown by some nuns in the civil rights struggle: "God bless them, they haven't learned enough theology to rationalize themselves out of a holy obligation."

Anyone long associated with civil rights has been plagued by the writings of thinkers who do not intentionally rationalize themselves out of a holy obligation, but who reason toward some painful distortions. This may not indicate aberrations in their methodology, but simply an abys-

Selma, March 10, 1965

58

mal ignorance that leads them into judging black men as though they were imitation white men. This is perhaps why too often we hear them express high-minded and highly reasoned analyses that may "make sense" but are ultimately false and thereby ultimately cruel in their effects, though such an intention is wholly absent. No matter how flawless their method, their judgment simply fails to meet the basic test of reason which demands that a judgment conform to reality before becoming the premise for further reasoning.

Due to the duality of viewpoint, it is virtually impossible for such thinkers to make their judgments conform to a reality that is also the black man's reality and that takes into account all the nuances of black oppression. Any theology that ends up justifying, for whatever reason, the racist suppression of any man or group of men, is not a Christian theology, and its conformity to reality will be only to a fragment or an aspect of reality. Black theologians go even further: ". . . to deny the reality of black oppression and to affirm some other "reality' is to deny Christ. Through Christ, black people have come to know not only who he is but also who they are, and what they must do about that which make them nothings."[15] Black men simply reject any theological equivocation on this point and call it "the work of the Antichrist."[16] The fact that many white churchmen are unaware

of this, possibly unaware even that there are "reasoning" black theologians, is only another indication of the quality and the time lapse in our perception of what is happening in the black world. Black men grow tired of hearing words of white (rather than human) wisdom uttered tomorrow, as though they were new, by white thinkers ignorant of the fact that black people have often already meditated on them and disposed of them a year ago, or two, or ten.

For approximately a decade black Americans persevered in the dream of nonviolent resistance. But the success of nonviolent resistance always depends on the conversion of the hostile force. To succeed, it must "bring about a transformation and change of heart." The whole world was moved by the attempts of black Americans to accomplish this task, but white racists were not generally moved. An indication of the dehumanizing character of racism on racists themselves is surely found in this failure of love and redemptive suffering to cure the wounds of racism. Nonviolent resistance appeared to have failed. White men generally did not show any significant "transformation and change of heart." In fact, racists redoubled their efforts in the name of patriotism and Christianity, to suppress not only black people but all nonracists.

I personally feel that nonviolent resistance did, in fact, make profound changes in that it did touch and move many individuals privately. But these changes were intimate, surrounded by confusion, filled with fears of reprisals and character assassination. No one wants the disesteem of his fellowmen. The racists were quick to hurl charges of "nigger-lover" or "bleeding-heart" or "do-gooder" or "Communist" at any man who spoke reasonably. Thus many men, genuinely affected by nonviolent resistance and distressed by the barbarism of racists, were changed. Rarely were they changed deeply enough. A kind of sympathy and pity replaced their former apathy or indifference, or hostility. Most continued to regard black men as "intrinsically other" and failed to understand or repudiate the system of contradictories. It was a time when many who did see clear were praying that the white man would learn to love before the black man learned to hate.

Then, at a time when black men had grown tired of the beatings and the jailings and the continued violence practiced against advocates of nonviolence, when hope in "the white man's Christianity" had reached a low point, word came into the black world that two white nuns had publicly protested discrimination in Chicago. These Franciscan Sisters, criticized by white Christians and coreligionists, could hardly have known how many black men

watched and talked: "Maybe some of those white Christians really do believe. . . ."

Hope rose again with Selma, a high moment in the history of civil rights in this land. Religiously identifiable men and women—priests, nuns, seminarians, rabbis, ministers of many denominations and laymen of many denominations—came to Selma by the thousands. Matt Ahmann of the National Catholic Conference for Interracial Justice almost exhausted himself and NCCIJ's funds helping to organize a reputable representation at Selma, seeing it as an opportunity to mitigate some of the scandal of white Christianity's apparent condoning of racism. Religiously identifiable men were no longer merely saying good things from safe places. No, they came and put their bodies where their mouths had been. In Selma, white martyrs were produced and black men saw that "the white man's God" could lead him to action and to sacrifice. No matter how much Selma was resented by white Christian racists, no matter how recalcitrant local Alabama church hierarchies showed themselves to be, Selma was a crucial and overwhelming demonstration that some white Americans were willing not only to talk about principles but to stand up and die for them.

Yes, hope was high in Selma. It is clear now that black Americans for long years lived on a dynamism of lifted hopes in high periods like Selma, followed by quashed

*Mathew Ahmann,
former director of
National Catholic Conference
for
Interracial Justice.*

hopes in low periods of backlash and apathy. For black Americans, fluctuation between hope and despair has, until recently, *depended on the moods of the white majority*. We know now that this has been the danger and the weakness and the shame of the black citizen's position in our society. But in those days we had to work within this framework. Alternatives had not yet appeared. The only apparent solution lay in the conversion of white America, in the hope that white America would rid itself of racist mythology, come to see clearly the contradictories of the "system" and repudiate the injustices of the system.

To put it bluntly: in those days the only way black men could hope for freedom and equality lay in pleasing the white majority into actions that would bring about an end to oppression.

The 1964 civil rights legislation gave new hope that perhaps this was being accomplished. Finally all the old WHITE ONLY signs were removed from public places.

But these were primarily external changes—important, yes—but not touching the core problems. For black and white men, the WHITE ONLY signs were symbols of racism. They were the external signs of an internal malady. Their removal made physical life less a problem for black men; made it less barbarous for a black man to satisfy his needs of hunger, thirst and elimination.

But these inconveniences had never been matters of prime importance. It was not walking many blocks to find a place where a black man could get a drink of water or food or use restroom facilities. Those are physical inconveniences and the merely physical has never been the important part of racism—the important part has been the psychological damage that occurs when a man stands always before his fellowmen and is viewed as the intrinsic other.

As a black man, perhaps a college professor (because it really did not matter whether you had high degrees or were illiterate) you might, in the old days, walk into a drugstore in New Orleans, make a purchase and be treated with perfect courtesy by a young white lady behind the cash register. You might then ask, as I once did when I was black, "Pardon me, but I am diabetic. Could you tell me the nearest place where I might find some water?"

You might then stand there and, with growing sickness, watch that sincere, kind and concerned young lady ignore a soda fountain three steps to her right as she carefully gave you directions to the nearest "colored" drinking fountain seventeen blocks away. She was no redneck bigot. No, she was a concerned young lady who was certain she had no prejudice. If you suggested to her that it was cruel to send a human being in need for water seventeen blocks when water was available three steps away, she would have been crushed.

You knew that this young lady, formed by the "system" as all of us were in one way or another, limited and handicapped by that formation, saw only what was obvious—that you were "colored" and that the nearest drinking place for "coloreds" was seventeen blocks away.

It was not the seventeen blocks. That was nothing compared to the real and damaging offense. This was simply that you stood there as a man, as a human individual, and that this young lady viewed you always as the intrinsic other. Multiply this kind of incident thousands of times when black men have stood and still stand in the presence of "good whites" and are still viewed as "other," and it is perhaps easier to see why black men can be so burned not only by the redneck bigots but also, and far more often, by good whites who would never deliberately affront or offend them, but who do it constantly by regarding them as "you people."

And the same things occur everywhere and every day. Is the above any different from the treatment a black, middle-aged teacher received in a Michigan community when she went into an eating place, was courteously seated and served, but got the message when she forked into her omelette and found it so over-salted and over-peppered inside that she could not eat it. No one knew her, she could have been an educator or an illiterate, a saint or a criminal. It would not have mattered. In that restaurant, she was simply the "intrinsic other," and though the law would have prevented the restaurant personnel from turning her away, it did not prevent them from telling her, in this way, that "intrinsic others" were not welcome. Black people, even the most distinguished and famous, get this kind of "message" constantly.

So it was not the physical inconvenience that damaged so deeply. It was not even those old WHITE ONLY signs. When they were removed, the fundamental injury remained. A major part of the experience of blackness, unknown to most whites, has been that men stand in front of doors through which a man has to pass in order to be a man, doors over which WHITE ONLY signs have never been placed, and where black men have been turned away. Black men have never seen WHITE ONLY signs over the doors of churches to my knowledge. And yet one of the deepest and most sustained shocks I received as a black man came from standing in front of the doors of churches of many denominations, including my own, and being repulsed or given the stares because of my black skin, standing in front of the same churches that would have and in fact have welcomed me with open arms

as a white man.

The same kind of good whites who have showered me with smiles of welcome and friendship in churches when I was white, came and planted themselves in front of the same churches when I approached as a black man. And since racists always blame the victim, they spoke to me in this manner: "What are you trying to do—get yourself in trouble. You get on over to that nigger church where you belong and you cut out this foolishness." I stood there, as many other black men have stood before men who were protecting the "House of God" from my contaminating presence. I listened while inside men, women and children prayed and sang hymns to God. The first time that happened to me as a black man, the hymn being sung inside was called *Walking in The Path of Jesus.* I stood there burning, wondering if I had lost my mind or if they had lost theirs. This kind of thing happened consistently, not in rare and isolated incidences. And it is not limited to the South, either, as black people can everywhere testify. There is little point in naming specific churches and denominations. In many where church leaders have made superb proclamations, it happens.

Three years ago, at a midnight service in Duchess County, New York, a group of highly distinguished black men and women, guests of noted black composer and concert pianist, Dr. Robert Pritchard, were asked not to go to the communion table, "because there's a whispering campaign in the church. They say if the niggers go to the communion table, the whites will boycott it." Dr. Pritchard and his guests remained in their seats, but they gave the note to the minister immediately afterward. Instead of reading it to the congregation, which would surely have repudiated the writer of the note, he merely thanked them for "not having caused an incident." Was the situation corrected? Who can know? Dr. Pritchard and his family resigned from the church and would never go near it again, not because of the note, but because the minister appeared more concerned with "keeping things quiet" than with correcting a scandalous abuse.

If whites rarely hear of them, black people know about such things, overwhelmingly, and are faced with this contradictory: the churches' official positions, which are good, and the silent language of attitudes that does not get corrected in the church. Who can blame black men who have this kind of insult, this kind of "intrinsic other" insult, ground into their lived experience, for wondering how it is that bishops can be so unequivocal about "obedience to authority" in matters of birth control, for example, and so utterly lax about "obedience to authority" in the correction of racist insults and injuries. More,

black men are not so impercipient as to fail to see deeply the contradictories involved when priests and nuns and Protestant ministers are removed or corrected or suppressed when they become "too committed" to the correction of such evils. This happens, and it happens with overwhelming frequency. It is an open scandal to black men and to some white men who learn of it. Certainly it is no secret in the churches, though the churches have attempted to make it a secret.

Those who have begun to bring these things out in the open have sometimes been accused of "creating scandal." I respectfully answered one southern bishop that I had kept quiet for years, confident that when these matters were brought to the attention of the bishops they would be corrected, and they had not been. I was not creating scandal, I was merely reporting on a scandal that already existed and threatened to go on existing.

Who is behind these incidents? When brought to the attention of the bishops, the bishops invariably lament them, but as far as black men are concerned, the churches are just as foundered in the intrinsic other concept as society in general. No one approves of such incidents and attitudes and yet they remain essentially uncorrected.

The important point here is simply that black men have been standing in front of doors to our highest institutions: our places of learning, our places of healing, our places of worship, and our courts of law—places where no **WHITE ONLY** signs existed, and have not yet been viewed as human individuals. Because this persists, the old idea of the "good white" has tragically faded as a concept on which black people based hopes of true equality and fraternity.

From that fabric of anguish and disillusion black men began to lose the old dream of an integrated society and look for new alternatives. One thing must be clear: the history of the black man in this land has been a history of good solutions that were not met in good faith, leading to less-good solutions, and finally to even less-good solutions.

In employment, for example. The original ethic of black men was flawless. Black men said three things:

1. We do not want any black man hired for a job for which he is unfit, merely because he is black. That is tokenism and damaging.

2. We do not want any white man deprived of a livelihood in order to get his job for a black man.

3. We want no ceiling placed on a black man's opportunities for advancement because of his blackness.

It was only when that ethic was not met in good faith by employers in general that less-good solutions had to be advanced until finally an obnoxious "quota" system was proposed. The general public became then highly critical of the quota system, critical of black men for suggesting it, without ever seeming to realize that the quota idea was just as obnoxious to black people as it was to whites and that it came into being *only* because the better solutions were simply not met in good faith.

The same is often true with the new alternatives. Many black men, even the advocates of black power, of the "separate" nation within a nation, regret that the earlier dream of a united society did not bear the fruit of the dream and regret, too, that the gradualism that had once held promise finally threatened to stretch on into eternity.

THE ALTERNATIVES

WHAT NEXT?

70   As a personal observation, I regret deeply, as do many men, white and black, that attitudes have finally driven black men to abandon many of the old dreams we shared, dreams that were good; and to embark into this period of transition that so bewilders men, but in which we are beginning to see our first real hope.

I have long felt that at a certain level of tragedy, recriminations are no longer proper. They appear as a cheap kind of luxury for lesser tragedies. No one, black or white, really wants what has happened. Much of what has happened came from deeply implanted attitudes that men did not want and most often did not know they possessed. For this reason, I have tried, in this little work not to "attack" specific individuals or events that might focus attention away from an overview of the general movements of history. It is too late for recriminations and accusations. We are concerned with those imprisoning attitudes that dehumanize men, and destroy communities, damage children and taint our institutions; even those institutions that contain within themselves the solutions: the educational and religious institutions. In almost every case, the damage occurs because of the mutilation of the principles such institutions profess to espouse. We remember an old philosophical saw that warns: "The community that distorts any valid principle to conform to its own comforts, (its prejudices), will end up seeing that the principle has not been distorted, but that the community has."

We suffer in this land not because of the dream but because of the mutilation of the dream by men and groups of men who have sought to bend it to conform to their conveniences or prejudices, or through some expediency consideration.

How often have we seen religious leaders making decisions not so much on the basis of what is immutably right as on the basis of "what will happen if I do such and such," on the basis of expediency.

This led Father Fichter, as already mentioned, to remark: "We have failed to do what we knew was right out of a fear of what hypothetically might happen if we did it."

In April of 1968, Cardinal Dearden expressed his concern that the new Gallup poll indicated fifty-three percent of the people in the United States felt that religion had no place in this area of social concern.

"It's a disturbing figure, because it is nine per cent higher than the last poll that was taken on the subject," Cardinal Dearden observed. "I think it brings home to us a fact that is unpleasant but must be faced up to: —many people seem to salve their consciences and dull their sense of concern by saying, to themselves at least and to their neighbors, that this is strictly a political matter in which the church has no business. As long as they can hide behind as neutral a bush as political partisanship, it is going to be very hard to smoke them out. . . . Somehow, we must bring home with greater force than before the fact that there are strictly moral dimensions to the problem—dimensions which are so clearly moral, so unmistakenly religious that the church cannot evade speaking on them or being concerned about them. . . . There is something alike in the mechanism of racism and the mechanism of alcoholism in this sense, that it seems to create a genius for self-delusion. People who are infected by this disease can think of a thousand pretexts and reasons for acting as they do. Somehow they can delude themselves of the soundest motives and of the strongest possible convictions, and while they remain in this stage of self-delusion, we are never going to reach them. We are concerned here with basic issues. Justice is an element that is so fundamental that it seems inescapable; and on top of justice, all the other implications are bound up with our concept of love of our neighbor. The results of the poll were disturbing to me because they reflected a movement in the wrong direction. I was quite prepared for the fact that there would be many who would like to see the church confined to the sanctuary and the sacristy—that's a traditional problem. But I did not expect to see the figures mounting

as high as they did."[17]

The time lapse in perceptions between whites and blacks had become critical by 1967. White men, usually successful and "concerned," were still telling black men it was just a matter of getting an education and pulling themselves up by their bootstraps. Newspapers were still carrying stories about black men who "had earned acceptance" and were "highly respected" in their communities. I have heard such men in seminars give this kind of advice and encouragement to black men who had degrees, who were better dressed than the white men. I have seen such black men listen, their veins knotting with rage, oaths beginning to form on their lips while the white man went right along telling *them* about his "colored friends, dear friends."

White men looked at the exploding black communities, "blamed the victim" and asked "Where are the black leaders?" meaning where are the "good blacks," meaning where are the "docile, reasonable black men of the past?"

"The problem is that we don't have any white leadership," said Father James Groppi.[18] "The reason why the Youth Council had to march for over 200 days in the city of Milwaukee is because there was no white leadership. Above all, there is the church. The church would not come forth and tell its white parishioners, 'Now, it's sinful for you to discriminate. It's right

THE CHURCH AND THE BLACK MAN

that we have a fair housing bill. You should go to the polls and you should inform your aldermen and you should inform the mayor of the city of Milwaukee that this is right and just.'

"There is much talk about the individual who is out in the street throwing bricks. I look at him and I know him. I feel like this myself very often. You know, you keep pounding on the door, trying to break down barriers of discrimination. The door keeps slamming shut. You get to a point where you want to go home and get a club. I mean this."

The selective hearing of the prejudiced who do not know they are prejudiced. White Christians hear Father Groppi speak as he did above and are repelled because here is a man who "condones violence," they say. If white children were involved, they would see it clearly as the children "fighting for their rights."

We met a young lady, eight years old, who had been arrested "a number of times."

In the juvenile court, the judge asked her, "What were you doing out the night you were arrested? Were you causing trouble?"

Father Groppi described it. "She looked at that judge, stood up on her own two feet and said, 'Causing trouble? I was out there plugging for my constitutional right of freedom of speech and the right of freedom of movement in this country.' The judge, who was not from Milwaukee, looked at her and said, 'Case dismissed.' "

Father Groppi also described police harrassment against black people, harrassment that exists in many areas and does not offend white people who learn of it. This harrassment can range from constant surveillance, stopping people in the street to ask "Where are you from?" or "Where are you going?"

"What happened to one the other night. A policeman stopped the car and put his rifle out of the window, patted it on the butt of the gun and said, 'Nigger, this is for you.' "

That is not violence? A part of our duality of viewpoint lies in this refusal to see the institutionalized violence practiced against black men (and other minorities), but to see quite clearly and label as "violent" the actions of men who stand up and fight against the injustices that surround him and damage him and his family.

It is not for nothing that minorities come to consider the police as "the enemy." Toynbee has said that if we do not learn the lessons of history we are condemned to repeat its errors. Without being pro or anti police, certain patterns are self-evident. One is that the police are just as afflicted as anyone else with the handicap of the "intrinsic other" concept. Police who are members of one ethnic group tend to develop prejudices against the members of

Rev. James Groppi, arrested in Milwaukee, 1967

other ethnic groups if they function in an area not of their own ethnic background. The Irish-American policeman in an Italian or Slavic or any other ghetto, since he deals with criminal elements, and since most crime in a ghetto is committed by members of the ethnic group inhabiting the ghetto, tends to view the "Italians" or whoever as lower criminal types by ethnic characteristic.

We hear talk today about the high crime rate among ghettoized black Americans, as though it were an ethnic characteristic. In the 1850's, we heard the same kind of talk about Irish-Americans in New York state, at a time when the Irish suffered massive discrimination in employment and housing and accommodations. Then, it was contended that sixty-eight percent of major crime in New York was committed by the Irish. The 1863 Hell's Kitchen riot in New York involved an explosion of resentment from the Irish. It was worse than any of the so-called riots we have known in recent years of exploding black resentments.

A year before the killing of Martin Luther King, we were in a terrifying position in this country. Rage meetings were being held in black communities, usually following some local scandal involving apparent attempts to harrass black people to a strike-back, involving rumors to create tensions, involving confrontations. I described such meetings in these terms:

A young man speaks. Only occasionally does he address me directly.

"Take ten," he calls out.

"Take ten," the others intone.

"Take twenty. Thirty's better—make up for somebody that can't get his ten."

Whether the meetings are held in Kansas, California, New Jersey or Michigan, the liturgy is similar. "Take ten."

Young men call it out in jovial voices, on the streets, in the supermarkets. "Take ten." The white world thinks they mean "Take a ten-minute break."

They don't. They mean there are ten whites for every black and before the whites kill the blacks each black should take ten whites with him.

A black man, middle-aged, well-dressed, a minister, leans to me and whispers: "You'd better listen. They're the ones that are calling the plays. They're saying it. You listen."

"Does the white American love the Nazis? He acts like it. The Nazis killed six million Jews. The Jews didn't know what was happening to them. They didn't raise a finger. Well—FOOL!—do you think we're going to go like that? Do you think we don't know? We're going to take ten."

"Amen, Brother," the others call out.

"Hell! Let's stop resisting the draft. Let them send us to Vietnam. Only when we get there, let's not shoot that yellow man out front. We can take our ten right there

alongside us."

Silence.

"The snipers have been told not to hit anybody. We haven't wanted to hurt the white individual—just the power structure. Now some big fat white-ass mayors are telling their police and the guard to shoot to kill. Now our snipers are going to shoot to kill. Any town where the white leaders want to exterminate us—and that's all it is, just extermination—there's where we've got to shoot to kill and each of us take ten or twenty."

"Amen. . . ."

"They can't say we haven't tried every other way."

The older men, the well-dressed older men added their *amens* to that.

"Now this is the *only* way left. They're talking about us DEPRIVED. Hell, I go to college. I was holding down two jobs when they picked me up. Yeah, they picked me up. I didn't have anything but a stick and a stone on me. They beat me on the way to jail. They sprayed insect repellent in my eyes. They messed up my wrist, and all the time they were saying 'You ain't hurt, nigger, Bop! You all right. Bop! Then the next day they released the white fellow who was down in our area shooting up the houses—turned him out on a thousand dollar bond, not a scratch on him either. And they let me out on a *five* thousand dollar bond—and don't you know they told me to go and be good!"

"Sure. Sure." the others said.

"And no white man—no church group —nobody said a thing. They don't care."

I have been attending these meetings all over this land, listening, mute.

I am asked: "What do you say to such young men?"

I don't say anything. I listen. What can you say? An older burned-out black man said to me not long ago when he took me into one of these meetings. "If you have to talk, don't say anything pious. We can't stand to hear the white man say another pious word."

What words are there to speak to a young man who tells me in an agonized voice: "A year ago I knew right from wrong. They treated me like a mad dog. Now, I'm sorry to say it, but if I walk into some supermarket and just one man or woman looks at me that certain way, or calls me 'boy' or 'nigger,' then I'm going to fix him so he can't see the sky. A year ago the thought of hurting *any* man would make me shake all over and want to vomit. Now, I'd kill him and then I'd just mosey back to the pool hall—it's the only *goddam* place we got to go—and my hand wouldn't even shake when I put that eight ball in that side pocket."

These meetings are not few, they are many. And they are attended not only by the young, but also by older men, even by prominent older men who have finally been driven to give up any hope that the white man will ever see, will ever act in good faith. One point is seldom understood by whites: Most black people hate the solutions to which the "white structure" drives men. Black people think whites are blind not to see the total triumph of the white racists.

Whenever a disturbance occurs, it is automatically assumed in the white press, the white community, the white Congress that it has been set off by blacks, probably by "outside agitators" who come in and stir up the good local black people. But a quite different pattern is emerging, one already well known to the black people. In many riot areas the patterns are almost identical. Usually late in the evening, city officials will be warned that a neighboring community has been reduced to flames and that carloads of blacks are converging from that neighboring area to destroy the city or town. The leaders prepare without checking, because the warning always comes late, the danger is immediate. Riot controls are put into effect. The white community arms itself. This has happened in many widely diverse areas: it was the pattern in Mansfield, Texas (Northside Fort Worth reputed to be in flames); in Wichita (Kansas City in flames and 250 carloads of armed Negroes coming to destroy Wichita); in Cedar Rapids (Des

Moines in flames, etc.). In some cities panic is intensified with the rumors of atrocities: a white lad has just been castrated by two Negroes, though the white lad is never named or placed in evidence. The police, the guard, armed and under tension, prepare to face the "enemy." All it takes then is for a few men to drive through the black community shooting off guns or stoning houses. Blacks pour out, sometimes as in Wichita only with stones and sticks. They are picked up, unjustly they feel and the "riot" is on. Blacks believe and so do I, that white racists trigger these holocausts; but from the white "investigators" and press, the same story emerges: sedition, the whole thing was carefully planned within the heart of the Negro community. This is only one of the reasons black men feel that white racism is triumphant and that blacks don't really have a chance anyway, so why not take the whole thing with them, leave the whites nothing.

Men who consider themselves "good whites" remain silent in such areas, often because they do not perceive the patterns (which seems suspicious, indeed incomprehensible, to most black people). The silence—no matter what the cause—is viewed as a condoning silence by black people.

Black men have meetings where outraged victims speak to the chorus of *amens*. Parents sit silent while their sons show their scars. The white man will break all the laws in the book to keep Negroes down, they say. The white man thinks we are fools. The white man's crimes against us go unpunished. Mountains of evidence pile up. The churches are silent. The schools send white-assed sociologists. We ask for bread and the white man feeds us a committee. We *demand* justice and we get a committee. Self-determination, God, the white man even has a committee to see how much self-determination HE's going to give US. It vomits out. Sedition? "You drive us crazy," Dr. Nathan Wright said, "and then when we act crazy you call it sedition."

That evening I went back into the white world and gave a lecture and heard the questions asked by white men, good white men, sincere and troubled white men. And I wished there were no black people in my audience because the questions asked by good white men now often drive blacks into a frenzy.

A young minister stood up. "Well, Mr. Griffin, you have presented the problem very well, but I would like to have your ideas on what we, as Christians, can do to help?"

A black man, a national director of NAACP, sat on the stage beside me. I saw his hands knot and heard him whisper, "Christ."

After that meeting, which the black men and I had attended in the afternoon, the question that made sense to the minister sounded strangely irrelevant to us. I could almost hear the groans of the black people in the audience. I felt like saying: "Form a committee." I felt like giving him Thomas Merton's answer: "Before you do a damned thing, just *be* what you say you are, a Christian: then no one will have to tell you what to do. You'll know."

Instead, I gave him an even poorer answer: "You ask what we, as Christians can do? First we have to recognize that we *didn't*. There isn't any time left to start. But we are still obligated to go on and act as though there is. We still hear the voice of outrage over the actions of black men. We still do not hear any similar outcry from Christians or others against racist crimes."

I left it there, not a good answer, feeling that almost any answer I could give was as irrelevant as the question had seemed. How could I make the young minister taste the fetor that poured out of black men's souls at such meetings. How could I make him feel the terrible nausea of black men driven to "give up" on white men and white men's Christianity.

And black men were driven to it, though we whites, never having perceived patterns, see only the final result. For example, all white men know of Stokely Carmichael, and most cringe with distaste at the very

name. He represents "dangerous attitudes" to white minds. What most whites do not know is that many black people also feel he represents "dangerous attitudes," but black people at least understand how he came to be driven to those attitudes.

What few whites realize is that for years Stokely Carmichael—a man of great insights—was a flawless advocate of nonviolent resistance: not only was he an advocate, he lived nonviolence heroically. For years when he was slapped down, insulted, jailed and abused, he would fall on his knees and pray for those who abused him. For years he prayed for the dehumanized white who loathed him for the unforgiveable sin of not being a "good nigger," for not grinning and yessing the way a "good nigger" should. Finally, when he could take no more, he was driven to become the Stokely that most men know today.

A few weeks prior to the killing of Martin Luther King, black men had begun to see the similarity of the patterns of detonating violence in the cities. Black men began to believe that these were not just "explosions," certainly they were not "planned from within" and they were not the result of "travelling black agitators," because such men, if they appeared at all, appeared after the explosions. Black men began to believe that these explosions were detonated by white racists. White men were involved in all of them as detonating factors. Black men realized that "a handful of white men can blow any ghetto."

Father Groppi felt that the racists' use of the police as a deliberate harrassing element to drive black people to strike back so that they could be eliminated or suppressed "in self-defense" was a major ingredient in the tensions sustained in Milwaukee.

Create a climate of tensions in the black area, start rumors that will cause white men to arm themselves, set off the detonation by driving black men to a strike-back, then you can suppress the black man in the reputable guise of self-defense. This is the way black men came to view the patterns, and the way many whites came to view them also.

Create chaos, then any racist can come in as a knight in shining armor, promise to "do whatever is necessary to restore law and order."

This was the pattern of the Nazis in the beginning.

Black people saw the similarities. White men also saw them. The former Governor of Pennsylvania expressed great concern at the similarities in a long conversation with me.

Black leaders began to spread the word in the ghettos. Don't let them drive you to a strike-back. You are playing into their hands if you continue to fall for this

Chicago, November, 1967

technique.

The patterns were understood. They made sense now to black men, even if they were obscure to most white men, including church leaders.

The killing of Martin Luther King could have sent this country up in flames if the patterns had not been understood by black men and if black men had not already spread the word. As it was, we escaped that open conflict between black men and white men. But the simmering ideas of black power that had been introduced as an alternative to "the dream of integration" now began to boil to the surface, to the distress of most whites who equated black power with violence, with "the black menace."

Black thinkers, black philosophers—usually quite unknown to white America—began to structure and analyze the weaknesses of black America—and since their philosophical analyses conformed to the black American's lived experience, much of it was immediately understood.

Hard as it was to swallow, it became evident that the old dream of an integrated society had been a weakening dream for black men. White America had continually rejected the dream and if you looked at it realistically, would go on and on rejecting the dream by refusing to see black men as anything but "intrinsically other" and by demanding that black men conform to white, middle-class cultural values, or become imitation whites. To make it in this society, black men had to "act white," which implied hiding or denying negritude, blackness, "niggerness" (as some black men now call it). It implied denying one's roots. Its success depended on winning white society's approval, on pleasing white society. Black thinkers began to refer to this as the problem of "fragmented individualism." The black man, to make it in the white man's world, had to detach himself (or pretend to) from his black origins, roots, culture. He had to "wear a white man's mask." He had to become fragmented, draw away from what was black, care about what the white man thought of him. He had to "act." What is more, it was self-defeating because no matter what he did, it would never be enough. White society promised to continue "drawing the line." That line might be drawn at the bank when he sought a home loan or a loan to expand his business.

How do you counter this fragmented individualism? By recognizing the reality of its weakening and indeed impossible aspects and by deliberately returning to a Brother and Sister concept, by refusing to hide negritude, by taking words like *black* and bringing them out in the open and hammering them home until they lost their negative tones and became words of pride and beauty, by refusing to wear the "white man's mask," and on the contrary, taking the seeming disadvantage of blackness and turning it into an advantage.

This was the beginning of a sweeping change in black thinking and black ideas— it spread so rapidly that white men could not keep up with it unless they were closely tutored or deeply involved with the black man's problems of white racism. Even black people who were frightened by the term black power, were swept along with the philosophical revelations of black power thinking.

Black power rose to the surface at a time when this land faced a confrontation that appeared inevitably to lead to violence and to genocidal suppression of black America. Black power rose, if men could only perceive it, as almost a stroke of genius that could avoid that violence, that could turn the burning resentments and the energies they engendered, into healthful and constructive channels.

Black power, thus understood, implied not the advocacy of violence, as so many whites think, but the alternative to that kind of fruitless confrontation.

"The typical white response to black power is the feeling that this is a threat and that we are in danger and that it denotes violence and hatred," said Reverend Albert Cleage.[19] "Really, the argument used today in terms of the violence as opposed to nonviolence is really not a valid argument. Violence or nonviolence is simply irrelevant."

This whole matter of violence or non-violence has come to a head as an immensely ironic part of the duality of viewpoint in the black world. Black people are surrounded by armed white camps. White men everywhere have been arming themselves, forming civilian posses, doing this in the great American tradition of a man's right to defend his home and property and family. Let a black citizen do precisely the same thing and this is termed "advocating violence." Black people, many of them, have learned from white people. Black people will defend themselves. ". . . we were rather weird creatures in America dedicated to nonviolence in the midst of a nation as violent as America is, has been, and will be."

Black power concepts and history have been well discussed in books dedicated to the subject, so we can only summarize them. Black power is an alternative to the dream of an integrated society. If the dream of an integrated society has been fulfilled, them Black power would be useless and indeed could not exist.

For four hundred years, the dream has been an integrated society. Black men were dedicated to the American dream. Black men really believed that it would be possible for white men to put aside prejudice. All black hopes and actions were directed

James Henry Rollins, black militant of St. Louis

to the one dream. Almost all black organizations were integration organizations.

Black people, suffering the disadvantages of separation dreamed only of integration. If a black business started up, black people would refuse to "buy black." After all the years blacks had worked for integration, they would not self-segregate in business, in block-voting for black candidates, in any manner that would hinder the dream of the integrated society. As a result, it was impossible to build strong black organizations or to garner economic strength or political strength.

"We believed there was coming a day in the not too distant future when black people would be integrated into the mainstream of American life, and we didn't want to be the one to put up any barrier to block this kind of integration," Rev. Cleage observed.[21] "So, the dream of integration served for almost four hundred years to *block* any meaningful activity in the black community. Now, at the same time we were separate in a very real sense. We were separate in every aspect of our lives. Even as black people said to each other, and black people often said it, 'I don't believe in anything all black,' everything they knew, everything that existed for them was all black." This was due to a white imposed separation. If a black man tried to move out of the ghetto, connivance on the part of real estate agents

and lending agencies placed impediments in his path.

"We were separate and yet we dreamed of integration and therefore did not utilize the separation for our benefit. We permitted the separation to be utilized for our exploitation."

In recent years, the dream of integration began to crumble. It began to crumble as white men who spoke in favor of that eventual dream acted in a way to oppose it.

"You remember the scenes on television when we were seen every night at the six and eleven news, where white people were using violence to destroy the efforts of black people in their confrontations to demand integration. Black people would demand integration of a lunch counter, and all the hatred and violence of the white people would be brought out." Gradually black people began to realize that opposition would meet every step the black man made toward integration.

The confrontations "forced people throughout America to see that white people did not want integration, that white people will not accept integration, that white people will fight against integration—violently, as violently as they feel it necessary to prevent it, to block it, to thwart it." So black people began to change their own conceptions about the reality of any hope of an integrated society.

One of the ironic consequences of

Martin Luther King's ministry lay in his genius for confrontation, allowing black men to see white racism unmasked.

"Black people had a kind of storybook conception of white people. And black people tended . . . through this period to feel that every disadvantage that black people endured in America was our own fault. We always had the idea that if we could measure up, if we could learn to talk right, to dress right, and to look right and to look as much like white people as possible, then white people would accept us. And if white people didn't accept us, then there must be something wrong with the things we were doing. We never blamed white people, we blamed ourselves. But gradually during this recent period, we came to look at white people realistically as we were never really able to look at Ol Massa on the plantation or the Klan as they rode in the South or the exploiters in northern cities. We began to just look at white people honestly and see them like they really are—a people who are dedicated to maintaining white supremacy by any means necessary, willing to use any kind of violence and any kind of subterfuge, any kind of illegality, anything at all to maintain white supremacy."

If such words affront white men, it tends to prove the duality of viewpoint. Certainly no one can look closely at the events of the past years and fail to understand the black man's growing disillusionment with the dream. Even Martin Luther King admitted that the subsurface community racism hardened and came to the surface every time an attempt was made to desegregate. For a time black people entertained the illusion that "most bad whites were in the south and most good whites were in the north." It was really again, Dr. King, who made black people lose that illusion, when he moved his activities from the South into northern cities. There the very white men who had so praised his work in the South, offered him the same kind of opposition in their own cities that he had received in the South.

"The actions of Dr. King's movement in Chicago demonstrated beyond a shadow of a doubt that the opposition which black people find to integration in the North is more complete, is more sophisticated, is more dedicated and more violent in the North than in the South. Dr. King made no progress whatsoever in the city of Chicago. The total white structure came together to see that nothing could happen in Chicago. And then we saw the march into Cicero. . . . In Cicero we saw the same faces of hatred, the same violence, the same dedication to white supremacy in the North. So for black people throughout America the complete dream of integration was shattered. Integration was through. White people had destroyed the dream, the myth, the

Martin Luther King at Chicago "Summit Meeting," August 17, 1966

hope—it was gone."

Black men stopped dealing with the hope and began to face the reality that was apparent to black people: the reality that the white man in America was going to go on maintaining the separation that had always existed: that men had better start dealing with that reality. Black separatism is a misnomer, since this is merely the black man's recognition that white-imposed separatism is the reality and that it is not going to vanish in the near future.

Until this change took place, black men were dealing in a dream of the future. The change involved dealing with the reality of the present.

First, as has been mentioned, there was the problem of a community of fragmented individuals. "Each black person was an individual to the extent of total sinfulness—no sense of brotherhood, no sense of relationship to his own people."

The way was to talk unity, to talk and think and feel the brother and sister concept, to stop trying to escape from the black brothers and sisters into that white world, but to unite and try with the brothers and sisters to do battle against "this vast white sea of oppression which is destroying me." Concern among black men moved from concern for the individual into concern for changing conditions that affect the lives of black people.

With this came the growth of what philosophers termed "black consciousness" which began to open doors into the rediscovery of black history, of Africa, of basic origins and a redefinition of Christianity.[21]

"So there is black consciousness, there is a growing sense of black pride, and there is the knowledge that (fragmented) individualism is the destruction of black people."[22]

"In terms of organizational structure, black people are beginning to build caucuses in every organization, in every church group throughout America, on a sense of unity that stems from a knowledge that we are a separated people and live a separated kind of existence and that we have to use that separateness and come together in some kind of unity. So every religious group has built a black caucus of one kind or another. Every political group has a black caucus where black people no longer go in and seek to escape or lose themselves in whiteness, but look around and see if there are any black brothers and sisters so we can come together for the benefit of black people—not for the benefit of ourselves as individuals, but for the benefit of all black people; with the feeling that if we can't utilize this situation, this organization, this structure, this church, this political organization, for the benefit of all black people then we have no business in it."

And very significantly, Rev. Cleage

adds: "Black people are not only evaluating the organizations and structures and churches they are in, coming together in black caucuses so that they can work together, but coming together with the implicit determination that if this institution or organization is not for the benefit of black people, then we have to get out of it."

Black power involves restoring to the black man's dollar its full use and full value. "We don't have millions of dollars to build with, but we have millions of people with a few dollars who can put their dollars together." Black men have come to realize that through the old refusal to buy selectively, their dollars usually went out through the white-owned chain stores in the black ghetto, into white banks that then were selective (on a racial basis) in making loans to black men in the areas of housing and business.

To salvage this dollar, selective patronage makes more and more sense. Not only selective patronage but a demand that the store in the black ghetto hire black employees and further that it bank the profits from the operation in a black bank, preferably, but at least in a bank that has proven it does not discriminate in its lending policies.

Black power involves using the vote. The white man has simply run to the suburbs, leaving the black man in the inner-city ghettos. As a result in many cities now having a predominantly black inner-city population, black mayors and city councils can be elected.

In the matter of education, black power philosophers have perhaps the deepest impact on black people as a whole. The black child in a school with a standard white curriculum can very well come to the conclusion that the only heroes in history have been white. It is clear now to most black parents that they must immediately salvage the black male child's image of the black man as a being capable of dignity and heroism. The death of the image of the black male as a fully self-determining, accomplishing, creative and contributing member of society, comes early in the male child. It comes from the fact that the system, as we have seen, contrived to destroy the black male's sense of his masculinity; from the fact that in an essentially patriarchical society, the system has made black society a matriarchical society. This is one of the most important aspects of black philosophy, one that has swept the black populace from every area: the determination now to salvage the self-respect in black male children by insisting that schools teach black history in which the accomplishments of black men are emphasized, the insistence that teachers stop perpetuating the image that everything the black man has accomplished has been through the leadership and benevolence of whites

(the superior leading the inferior).

Jonathan Kozol in his award-winning DEATH AT AN EARLY AGE has given us a magnificent study of the psychological death of black children in our schools where the thinking is geared to white goals and aspirations and white versions of history.

These perceptions have come so rapidly in the black world that whites are perplexed and bewildered by the sudden changes among parents and students. Black parents are marching on school authorities, demanding that the black child be saved from the psychological death. This has caused difficulties in all schools, including the inner city Catholic schools. The real difficulty at St. Dorothy's in Chicago where the newspapers simply announced that some of the nuns had walked out because of differences with black priest, Father Clement, came to a head over the fact that one of the nuns wanted to, insisted upon, having all the black children wear green on St. Patrick's day. To the black child and his parents (and certainly to many of the more percipient Sisters in that same school) this was a relic too degrading to be borne: making black children into fake little Irishmen at a time when black parents were trying to do everything to give children a pride in their blackness.

One of the moving things about this change came from the fact that white teachers, almost as much as black teachers, became concerned with the damage done to the black schoolchild. These things were part of the system. No teacher wanted them to continue. I was overwhelmed with requests from teachers who wanted seminars so they could learn what they were doing wrong and how they could help salvage the black schoolchild.

The Mott Adult Education Program in Flint, under the direction of a brilliant and remarkable black lady, Mrs. Marguerite Randall, and the Cleveland Public School System, under the direction of Dr. Briggs and his integrated administrative staff have done laudable work in this area of teacher education and the correcting of policies and curricula damaging to the minority child.

One of the things few whites, few educators and perhaps few blacks realized was that the black child, with his "separated" lived experience was simply not learning in the early grades of school anything that related directly to his experience and his problems. If he had artistic gifts, these might very well be discouraged because of the old stereotypes that said the black man was a laborer. His image of the black man had to be that of a man being led by the hand by some white man.

This is why students on college and university campuses changed, formed black student unions. Suddenly the black student

92 was no longer primarily concerned with the things of the past. This hurt and bewildered white students who in the past have helped fight a good fight for integration—often at great sacrifice. What the white student had not realized was that black students no longer cared about desegregating fraternities and social activities. No, the new ideal was to get as many black students on the campus as possible, learn everything relevant to the solution of the black men's problems and get on back to the black world to contribute to the move toward self-determination and manhood.

This did not mean that black students could not and would not form friendships with whites capable of relating: it meant that the image of the white man, student or not, leading the black man had to be abolished. It is true that when whites, no matter how sympathetic, join with blacks in support of any curative cause, there is an assumption of leadership on the part of the whites. For the sake of the black male image, that picture has to go, black men have to present an image of black self-determination. Deeply involved whites like Jonathan Kozol, Father Groppi and others have understood the supreme validity and importance of this.

Black men talk about these things frankly and openly today—another healthful sign. White men who still function in black areas play a new role. We support whole-heartedly the need for this new image of the black male as a man of dignity and self-determination. We seek the lesser places, and we seek to deemphasize the white hero role in matters of concern to black people. Father Groppi did splendid work with his youth group in Milwaukee and then backed out and left it to black people to continue. He has sought a black priest to take over as pastor at St. Boniface, offering to become the assistant. When we speak to school children, black and white, we obscure ourselves, explain why we do it, and emphasize the black heroes and martyrs (and there is no scarcity of them.) We try to build in the black child the new image, and we do everything to avoid the old one of the white man guiding the black man to the destiny white men have helped choose for the black men.

The attitudes of black students have caused great confusion. What must be remembered is that black taxpayers have probably put more dollars into education than has been taken out; that these are not perverse demands—the demands for courses relevant to the black man's lived experience; and that the key is in the matter of self-determination. White men who really perceive what these new attitudes are all about must surely see that supporting them is not only black America's best immediate hope, but also white America's best immediate hope.

Principal, Brother Joseph Davis, and staff member in ghetto Catholic school, Dayton, Ohio

94 This is one of the reasons black clergymen have tried to wake up the institutional church through the formation of black caucuses. Black priests perceived these changes as rapidly as other black men. They perceived also the duality of viewpoint that would make the white-dominated church lag far behind in arriving at an understanding of these new viewpoints, and as a result become even more irrelevant than before insofar as black Christians are concerned. Moreover, black priests, trained thinkers, were not being utilized by the bishops for consultation: the blackness of black priests was being thrown away by the Church. It is safe to say that with rarest exceptions, no white man can know the nuances of the black man's problems as well as black men can know them. Bishops usually call in specialists for advice. If there is an economic problem, they seek advice from economists. But with specialists already in their midst —the black priests—bishops rarely even consult them as specialists in this critical area where black men know that guidance is needed but where tragically enough Church leaders have rarely perceived the need for guidance. If black souls are not to be further and completely and hopelessly alienated and the Church simply kicked out of the ghetto, something drastic needed to be done. Black priests caucused, with the intention of trying to show the Church that black power is not the *threat* so many think

it is.

So far their voice has scarcely been heard. Their first statement to the bishops was not even acknowledged. Black priests are in the anguish of belonging to a church, of being priests of that church, and of knowing profoundly the patterns of alienation—and of not being heard: to the Church's great detriment. Other organizations are bringing black people in as consultants at the highest levels in decision-making processes, beginning to undestand the black man's critical need to have a self-determining voice in all decisions that affect him. The churches have not yet come to this. White men make the decisions, still, mostly in consultation with other white men.

Will the Church miss this last opportunity? Will the Church drive black people away because of the inability to see in time the depth of the need for curative action?

Separatism is a hard fact. The churches have not escaped the separatism (in this sense). Separatism was not imposed by black people but by white people. In all things, including religion, black men have a choice: they can permit this separatism which exists and which is forced upon black men by white society, to be used exploitatively (in the sense that it is used to deny black men self-determination); or it can be used constructively. Black men are no longer going to tolerate the exploitative use of separateness in no matter what institution, and we should thank God for that. The institutions that do not understand this and that continue to move in the old ways will have gained nothing and lost much.

Black people, even those who do not advocate black power and still dream of the integrated society, have been deeply moved by these changes.

"We will control our own community, and in this kind of self-determination, we will build a beautiful community in which black people can walk and live with pride and dignity."

"We have come to accept the new reality. The white man finds it very difficult to accept the new reality which we represent. We are not the same black people that you dealt with a few years ago. We are a new people and that makes a new reality with which you have to come to grips. We cannot go back to any kind of existence which does not give us power and control over our own destiny," Rev. Cleage said.

The key is there. The church that does not grasp it will have lost all chance of becoming truly universal and will become not the Church but merely the "white" church. White people must decide how they will react in terms of these new black concepts which are profoundly human concepts.

At the end of his address, a white priest disturbed by the implacability of Reverend Cleage's presentation, asked how he could reconcile the separateness with Christ's teaching of unity and brotherhood.

Reverend Cleage reminded him that it was precisely because white men had ordained and enforced separation that black men had been driven to these conclusions. He said black men did not desire the separateness that has been so damaging. He remarked that if white men had been preaching Christ's teaching of unity and brotherhood with any efficacity, the separateness would not exist as the reality it is.

If all of this sounds too negative, if there could have been any lingering doubts about failures of the churches *in the eyes of black men,* surely those doubts received a blow in April of 1969 when the National Black Economic Development Conference issued its demands for reparations from the churches in what has become known as the Black Manifesto. The decisions at the founding conference in Detroit sent a reverberant shock throughout the country. Black delegates to the conference voted 187-63 to seize "white Christian churches and Jewish synagogues" until such religious bodies gave $500 million in reparations to various black projects.

Presented by James Forman, the manifesto proposed disruption of churches and church-sponsored agencies until demands were met. Forman asked for "total involve-

Father August Thompson

ment" of all black people in pressuring "racist churches" to comply.

According to the manifesto, the $500 million would be used for such projects as a southern land bank to help people buy land; purchase of publishing and printing industries; four cable television networks; a research center for problems of black people; a national black labor strike and defense fund; a black university and a United Black appeal similar to the United Jewish appeal. The manifesto also called for a Black Anti-defamation League.

It asked whites to show "the patience, tolerance and non-violence" that have always been expected of blacks.

"We were kept in bondage and political servitude and forced to work as slaves by the military machinery and the Christian Church working hand in hand," the document stated.

The contents and tone of the manifesto deeply shocked many whites and blacks, but as the months passed, the demands have persisted and it is being taken more seriously. Washington and Detroit religious leaders have asked that representatives who come into churches to explain the Black Manifesto be received courteously and made welcome. At the time of this writing, a steering committee has been appointed —without yet indicating their acceptance —which includes officials of black caucuses among Catholics, Presbyterians,

Methodists, American Baptists and Unitarian-Universalists. The New York Archdiocesan chancery rejected the reparations demands. The Washington Square United Methodist Church contributed $15,000 and later Chicago's North Side Cooperative Ministry—an ecumenical group of twenty churches—pledged ten thousand dollars, but rejected "acceptance of the Black Manifesto in its entirety." The Episcopal Church has pledged an initial $200,000.

Again, it must be emphasized that black men do not think and act monolithically, but certainly the new reality is widespread among black Americans. What we can say is that almost all black men feel that white America, including white churchmen, are set in a kind of spiritual rigor mortis of racism, and therefore nearly all black Americans are now militant for goals of manhood and self-determination without necessarily being in agreement as to the methods of achieving this. Some black men favor black power concepts as the greatest hope. Others, in great numbers, still cling to the older hopes of reconciliation and conversion—all in being militantly determined that black men will be men.

To judge from the polls, black men across the land have rejected violence to a higher degree than whites. Studies made in the spring of 1969 and published in the *Detroit Free Press* indicated that only two percent of black Americans have gone

Father Ibe, a Biafran priest,
presently working in a black American ghetto

98 along with the advocates of violent disruption, while eighty-nine percent have rejected them. This does not mean, obviously, that some bungling, or some viciousness could not set off the cities again in holocaust.

Will the churches become aware of these new realities (and the causes) in time to salvage themselves insofar as this matter of racism is concerned? There is no doubt about what the churches are supposed to stand for in this matter.

Will white churchmen learn quickly enough through authentic church leadership so that encounters with black Americans cease to imply that the white men has something to concede to the black man? Above all will we learn to stop trying to turn black men into merely white Christians?

It can be done. It is still not too late. We have the resources to accomplish the task that will be healing not only to black men but quite especially to white men and to the Church itself.

No one really knows, of course. The signs are not very encouraging. Priests who become "too Christian" in this matter are still being removed. Nuns who do the Gospel's work too well and attach themselves too wholeheartedly to the causes of justice are being quietly transferred or suppressed. Some bishops, at least, continue to be wary of this kind of "troublemaker." The trends in Church and politics, from the point of view of racial justice, appear somber indeed to black people and to many whites. Religiously we see evidences of a regression back to the days before Vatican II. Politically we see evidences of a regression back to the fifties. We are retrenching at a time when we have so much to renew, so much to sacrifice in the matter of sacrificing the security of our cultural prisons and of opening ourselves to one another. Those churchmen, priests, nuns and laymen who would leave if the Church recognized the new reality and sought to implement and serve it —rather than impede it—must be allowed to go. If a stand on racism drives them out, they should never have been there in the first place.

The churches must help us see that our differences do not make us enemies. The differences could be an enormous enrichment if the racist Christian would ever stop running long enough to give them a chance to enrich, to humanize, to cure.

We leave this report open-ended with an epilogue of the greatest importance, largely prepared by Brother Joseph Davis, of the problems as viewed by the Black Priests' Caucus and approved by them. It is made available through the courtesy of Rev. Fr. Don Clark, President of the Black Priests' Caucus and Brother Joseph Davis, Vice-President of the caucus.

The Report of the National Advisory

Liberation School, Nashville, Tennessee

100 Commission on Civil Disorders spoke of the need for "new attitudes, new understanding, and above all, new will."

It concluded: "There can be no higher priority for national action and no higher claim on the nation's conscience."

If our wisdom and our resources, moral, intellectual, technical and spiritual can be directed to this "high priority" and to this "claim on the nation's conscience" then we can bring resolution to these problems in a victory greater and more historic than any moon landing.

Anything less will not be enough and we will have failed to bring resolution to a problem that plagues all men in all lands —and the churches will remain a mockery of "black" and "white" Christianity, which is no Christianity at all.

THE CHURC

ND THE URBAN WHITE

Epilogue I

By Mathew Ahmann

It almost seems unnecessary for me to address myself to the subject, "The Response of the Church to the White Crisis." It's been good to hear this year the many comments and concerns at this meeting about the responsibility of the Church to this problem. A year ago, most of you who work in the inner city were saying, "To hell with the white community." And there was a tendency to separate your service to the people in the ghetto from the problem of exploitative white power. Whether the change in your mood is due to the Kerner Report, or to your growing anxiety over the lack of a black Roman Catholic ministry and the growing shortness of your service in the ghetto, seems irrelevant. We seem finally to have realized that while we must serve to enhance black power, our primary strategy in doing this is to do something about our attitudes, values and structures of whites who stand in the way of equity for the black, brown and red communities.

Do you remember the words of the Kerner Report—

". . . Our nation is moving toward two societies, one black, one white—separate and unequal. . . . Discrimination and segregation have long permeated much of American life; they now threaten the future of every American . . . . This deepening racial division is not inevitable. The movement apart can be reversed. Choice is still possible. . . . Segregation and poverty have created in the racial ghetto a destructive environment totally unknown to most white Americans. . . . What white Americans have never fully understood—but what the Negro can never forget—is that *white society is deeply implicated in the ghetto. . . .*

"Certain fundamental matters are clear. Of these, the most fundamental is the racial attitude and behavior of white Americans toward black Americans. Race prejudice has shaped our history decisively in the past. It now threatens to do so again. *White racism is essentially responsible for the explosive mixture which has been accumulating in our cities since the end of World War II.*" (Emphasis added.)

The "Urban White" does not have a very good record in race relations.

Any psychologist could tell you that the urban white has a very inflated but insecure ego. The Church has taught him that his soul was washed "pure-white" with the waters of baptism, placed before him the image of a white Aryan Christ, helped nurture him from poverty to wealth, aided him to political power, domination of police and fire departments; by and large his political structures, his union structures, his corporate structures are as white as the structure of his Church. He thought he was doing good by abhoring the violence of racists in Little Rock, and he backed the bishop against Mrs. Gaillot in New Orleans.

It is obvious the Church did not learn enough from Little Rock or from New Orleans. Now the northern white mask is stripped bare. What shows forth in the media photos are the same ugly faces of hatred the righteous North had seen in the South. In fact, the long-held conviction of some observers that race relations were worse in the North than in the South is now self-evident. Still the mass of white Northerners say there is no race issue in the battle over neighborhood schools, or over union apprenticeships, and do not see themselves in the mirror. Racism in the North has given birth to a new species: white people have turned themselves into White people.

While it is a horrendous prospect, the violence of a Watts, or a Newark or a Detroit is nothing compared to the steady toll of arsons, beatings and shootings perpetrated by whites against Negroes since I have come to Chicago in 1952. I have before me the vivid pictures of whites clubbing Negroes in Chicago riots even in 1919. And Dennis Clark writes vividly of the violent Irish rebelling out of their poverty in New York's Hell's Kitchen in 1863, refusing to fight in the Civil War for "those niggers." Lincoln had to bring the crack Union troops from the front lines in the South to quell the Hell's Kitchen riot in New York —urban violence unmatched by any rebellion or riot of today. Whites have short

memories, indeed this memory problem should start clinical psychologists off to explore if this mental inadequacy is biologically determined.

No, there is less to be feared from the righteous wrath of an aroused Negro community than the steady, sinister, subtle violence of whites against Negroes, and now the open glaring hatred which drives whites to arms in Dearborn, Michigan, and with a sheriff in Chicago's Cook County.

If a small clique of new Negro anarchists cry violence, one must admit they have both learned it from a domineering white culture and been goaded to it by whites. For those in the Church who are concerned, it does little good to cry "law and order." The problem is to convert the whites, not the Negroes.

Some years ago white men came to North America from Europe and met an indigenous Indian population which could truly be said to own the land which is now the United States. These early explorers and military men accompanied by their missionaries and the colonizers who followed them, laid the base for an eventual national policy which has pushed the Indians from their land and all but exterminated them as a people.

Later on white men brought Africans to this continent in chains to use them as animal-like labor to help keep white civilization wealthy. Considered property by state

106 as well as Church (indeed not a few religious orders owned slaves) the white man did violence to these Africans who came to be known as Negroes, later "the colored" —Negroes again, and now in some circles, blacks.

Then in a burst of altruism underscored by agrarian economic necessities, President Lincoln hurled the North into a righteous crusade which included freeing the slaves, at least on paper.

But the whites were not to be put down. Within a few years they had fashioned a "reconstruction" in many Northern states as well as the South, and imposed radical suppression on the Negro community. Thus was laid the base for the virulent racism born in the United States which we see on the streets of the white community today. With ebbs and flows, challenged by some Negroes and whites from time to time, this virulent disease has built itself up into the white psychosis vibrating across the United States today, even affecting our relations with other countries.

Whites had a chance in 1963, when James Baldwin was the rage with THE FIRE NEXT TIME. But whites forgot and are now taking to the streets to defend their madness.

The President's Commission on Civil Disorders has come up with a solid package of badly needed programs designed to begin to meet the problems of the people in the ghetto. But scan the report from beginning to end and you scarcely find mention of a program designed to get at what the Commission itself calls the basic cause of the ghetto—white racism. Perhaps the Commission cannot be blamed, for it is true that racism is a kind of religion, and perhaps it is the Church which has to come up with the programs to get at it. Whites are a church-going people and we are facing a white schism.

The problem is on the doorstep of the Church too, because racial conflict in urban areas is frequently white Roman Catholics versus the Negro community. The most abrasive situations are almost invariably found in communities from sixty to eighty percent Roman Catholic. There are some exceptions, of course, even some cities which are exceptions. The suppression of the Negro community in Washington, D.C., is at this time largely by Congress itself, plus of course, the white suburbs encircling it like a noose.

I believe the Church will respond to the challenge of the Presidential Commission and put down schism in its own ranks as well. But it will call for sharp reappraisal of everything from our institutional structures (which are whiter than most large corporations) to our way of serving people in their neighborhoods.

One can sense the agony the white schism must be creating in the hearts of

108 "churchmen." In Chicago, for example, there is no doubt that a large segment of vociferous whites call Cardinal Cody a "nigger lover." Yet curiously enough many white liberals and Negro tacticians consider the Chancery Office part of the white status quo—that which must go if Negroes are to be free. The same problem is found in other cities around the country.

What does the Church have to do to tackle the white schism with more realism?

Leadership

There will be no possibility of healing the schism of racism within the Church by a schizophrenic approach to the problem. The Gospel does not permit the Church the freedom to please everybody. The Church, as expressed through leadership, programs, institutional behavior, must stand with the righteous demands of the Negro community. If this commitment to interracial justice is not clear in the minds of all, there will be no hope for reconciliation.

Secondly, we had better realize that healing the wounds, mending the schism, and meeting the needs of minority groups will be expensive. We must learn to pay for social action—more than the $40,000 budget of the Social Action Department of the United States Catholic Conference, or the modest general budget of the National Catholic Conference for Interracial Justice, or the undernourished race relations programs in many dioceses.

Structure and Personnel

As hard as it will be, we might as well face at the beginning that the recruitment and upgrading practices of the Church in the United States are as bad as those implied by the charges of discrimination the Presidential Commission lays against American business. The conscious or unconscious habits of the past and present in our dioceses and in most of our religious orders which keep Negro vocations to a minimum, and then do not give Negroes responsible decision-making positions in the administration of Church institutions, must be overcome by a large-scale deliberately planned program of the affirmative action. We must reach the point where the face of the Church reflects the universality of her doctrine. It is foolish to pretend that the Holy Spirit is not noving among Negroes, and that there are not vocations there for service in the priesthood or in religious life. The paternalism found in the approach of the Church to the Negro community, and the "Commission for the Catholic Missions Among the Colored People and the Indians" must be ended.

If whites can be made bishops at the age of 38, so can Negroes. Negroes must be given positions of responsibility in the administration of Church institutions, dioceses, religious orders and lay societies.

Related to this problem is the need, in overcoming benevolent paternalism as it

110 was recently called by all the Negro priests in Chicago, to establish ways to free Negro opinion in the Church, to let the opinions of Negroes rise to the surface, not remain suppressed or distorted as in the past.

There are large areas of many of our cities where the Church has never taught anything about racial injustice. These areas are increasingly the scene of conflict between whites and Negroes. In some dioceses an apparent decision has been made to try to do something about the problem in the white community even though it is late. Yet, many of the pastors do not sympathize with the position of the diocese—or their sympathies lie with the white racists. At best they frequently do not have stomach for the difficult fight which lies ahead. The diocese must be prepared to remove these pastors to get its program underway, or the policy will go down the drain.

Also needed are ways for institutional leadership to make contact with and develop relationships with leadership in the Negro community—not just upper middle-class leaders, but with a range of leaders including the tacticians on the streets. Catholic leaders I have observed seemed to have missed the great psychological shift which has been occurring in the Negro community in the past year or so. Since there is a much larger Negro ministry in most of the white denominations of Protestantism, the Negro-white confrontation

produced by this shift there has had great beneficial effect. The Catholic community has a bit of catching up to do.

One final point on personnel. There are some dioceses where the level of understanding, or present disposition of top Catholic leadership, will not permit the job to be done. Yet the race problem is so severe in so many cities, that this situation will call for some delicate work by the Holy Spirit and maybe even by Rome. It has been obvious that the Vatican has long been puzzled why the Catholic community in the United States looked so bad in race relations. Recent Apostolic Delegates, whatever else people say about them, have taken an interest in race relations. Frankly I hope that before policies for the election of bishops are established, Rome removes some bishops who stand in the way of any realistic approach to the problem of race relations in their communities. I am less familiar with the process of personal change in religious orders; there are some problems there, too.

The Education of Whites

Despite the white backlash, there is no doubt that since 1963 many whites were educated in good racial principles because, in confrontation with the Negro community, they *had* to make a choice. So any approach by the Church to the conversion of whites should recognize the need to encourage and protect the channels of expression needed by the Negro community. Those efforts of political systems or other community forces which try to suppress the new move toward power in the Negro community must be resisted. Negroes are merely doing what Pope John XXIII said all men should do—reaching out and grasping their rights.

Any effort to approach the white schism must involve a serious effort to train leadership—priests, religious and lay leaders. Enough has been done in various dioceses and denominations to enable others to learn from experience the major components of a first-rate leadership training program. Such leadership training must be a continuing program and must involve a confrontation with the energy and thought being developed in the ghetto.

The Catholic community can capitalize on its large school system—largely white in comparison with public schools. Through teacher training, the revision of white-biased curriculum materials, the introduction of the history of minority groups, a major contribution can be made to reach into the white community. There also have been some pilot programs to reach white adults through the school system which should be pushed as well. As an aside, it is patent that the large problems of public education in our cities will never be solved, indeed, cannot be faced frankly unless the complication of a large private parochial school system is faced. In one study it was demonstrated that the relationships between the public and parochial school systems actually served to widen the educational gap between whites on the one hand and Negroes and Spanish-speaking citizens on the other.

Religious orders have a significant opportunity to educate the trustees of their various institutions, and release the resources at the command of these trustees to meet the needs of the Negro community. Any appraisal of opportunity in this area should not neglect the fact that few Catholic institutions or programs have any Negroes or any poor people among their trustees.

The reform of the liturgy could be a powerful tool to reach white Catholics. I do not believe that the liturgy automatically results in changed beliefs or deeper commitment to love. But any liturgist working with a race relations expert could easily outline approaches to make the liturgy as an educator more powerful.

Specialized programs must be devised to reach more deeply into the white community to heal the schism. One must recognize that the ordinary structures of the Church may not function as usual in this area. Thus the mention earlier on possible changes. There are two fairly sophisticated programs in this area underway in various dioceses: Project Commitment and Project

112 Bridge.

Project Commitment is a broad leadership training program developed by the human relations staff of the Archdiocese of Detroit. It has recently become operative in several additional dioceses including Washington, D. C., and Cincinnati. Through a package of well-designed techniques it tried to help form the values of groups of Catholics on the neighborhood level. Still lacking is a needed program of follow-through utilizing the thousands trained in the program.

Project Bridge is presently a pilot program conducted in the metropolitan area and the Diocese of Cleveland. It is conducted by the National Catholic Conference for Interracial Justice and the American Council for Nationality Services in cooperation with the Cleveland Nationalities Service Center, the Diocese of Cleveland and the Catholic Interracial Council. A staff of seven are concentrating on building specific projects to bridge leadership among white ethnic groups and in the Negro community. Efforts range from beefing up existing diocesan programs (such as a Pulpit Exchange Program) in nationality neighborhoods, through community organization, to special efforts utilizing the mass media. On the basis of present interest it is likely that the Bridge program will spread into additional cities this year. My own feeling is that the best in Project Com-

mitment and the best in Project Bridge should be applied as quickly as possible in a large number of other dioceses.

There are more specialized or focused programs which need expansion as well. Perhaps the best of these is the Project Equality program already launched in 21 dioceses and in 89 Protestant, Orthodox and Jewish jurisdictions. Project Equality is largely aimed at an honest and sophisticated dialogue between religious denominations as purchasers and the business community in an effort to change white-biased personnel practices and open jobs for members of minority groups. Over 15,000 business firms are now involved in the program in some way. Project Equality is also aimed at the personnel practices of religious institutions.

Finally, no diocesan program will get anywhere with the white schism, unless it is given an adequate budget (no diocese has an adequate budget yet though several are pretty good), and a sophisticated staff which is in touch with and trusted by the range of leadership in the Negro community. This staff must be in touch with the central decision-making apparatus in the Catholic community, and other diocesan resources must be coordinated with its program.

Church Resources and the Negro Community

Any effort to reach the white conscience

must recognize that to the Negro community the Catholic Church is part of the "white system." An honest admission of this, and a determination to change, will recognize the sizable resources the Catholic community has which can be shifted out of the way so they don't block the Negro community, and shifted into programs designed to meet the needs of Negroes and members of other disadvantaged minority groups. The development of a vigorous, risk-taking program in race relations on the part of a diocese will do more than let the Negro community know where it stands. It will let the white Catholic community know that too, and this is a powerful educator.

Quickly, some additional problems and proposals. Someone said at this meeting, "We are playing games in the inner city because the suburbs are harder." I don't believe that we are playing games in the inner city, but from the point of view of necessary change, the suburbs are harder. The task of reaching those on the other side of the white schism (and schism it is —racism as a religion) is unglorious, unromantic and tough, and we must meet it with our best manpower. Secondly, I believe this predominately white denomination, the Catholic Church, has a useful service role in ministry to the black community.

First of all, if we are an inclusive

Church, we must reform our ministry. We must revamp our training programs and ordain black deacons and priests so we can fulfill what seems to me to be possibly our mission in the city—to somehow bridge the Negro-white gap. We are perhaps the one institutional complex which can make this bridge. Secondly, if we are an inclusive church, Negroes and Mexicans must be given visible positions of responsible decision-making in the Church. Thirdly, our service must be in response to the needs of the ghetto as defined by the ghetto. Monsignor Donahue's revamping of Catholic educational priorities placed education service in the ghetto first. The need is great, appropriate and urgent. We have skills and manpower which can flexibly help to meet the education gap in the inner city.

And also while every diocese should have Project Equality to bargain honestly for jobs in the white business community, we should go beyond this to help build economic strength. Our parishes, institutions, dioceses, can bank in the black community; our dioceses, parishes, institutions can buy everything from air travel to insurance in the black community. Construction to be built by the Church can be done by black construction firms.

Finally, I would hope that the Black Caucus would continue, not only for the needs of the black priests, but to help purify the rest of us. And the Catholic

116 Clergy Conference on the Interracial Apostolate and the Catholic Committee for Urban Ministry must quickly and realistically explore how they can work more closely together and organize more broadly and effectively. I would propose that we stop talking and staff and fund these two organizations. For our part, our offices will gladly donate space and auxiliary help.

In that framework, there are a variety of task forces which could go to work immediately. A number of them were outlined at CCIA last year in Chicago, but nothing has been done in the interim. The Black Caucus is obviously one. The task force on the dual parish system is obviously a second. We have freshly in mind the experience of one of the people attending this meeting who was in Selma, Alabama, where he was physically harrassed while attending what is still called "the white church" there.

Among many other task forces, there should be one on the suburban ministry. It must be recognized that the major mission of the Roman Catholic Church in the United States at present, the only way it can respond honestly to the Negro community, is to convert white people who now stand in the way of freedom for Negroes and whose racism is the basic cause of the ghetto and all the ills which flow from the ghetto.

If we believe in that ideal of an eventual open, integrated society, let us accept Rev. Albert Cleage's challenge and remove the myth against which the Negro community has been operating and change the white response to the black community, so an open society can become possible through the honest bargaining of equals with power to determine their own destiny.

THE POSITION OF
THE CATHOLIC CHURCH